I Bear Witness

Blessings!
Tim Maynard

Blessing!

George Muir

Tim Moyuan

I Bear Witness

A Memoir of Love, Loss, and the Goodness of God

BY
DR. TIM MAYNARD

I BEAR WITNESS:
A MEMOIR OF LOVE, LOSS,
AND THE GOODNESS OF GOD

Copyright © 2018

FIRST EDITION

ISBN: 978-0-9962685-8-5

DESIGNED & PUBLISHED BY:
Right Eye Graphics
311 Henry Clay Blvd.
Ashland, Kentucky 41101
(606) 393-4197
righteyegraphics.com

TABLE OF CONTENTS

DEDICATION:

TO PAM, MY SOULMATE

"RIGHT FROM THE START...
RIGHT TO THE END"

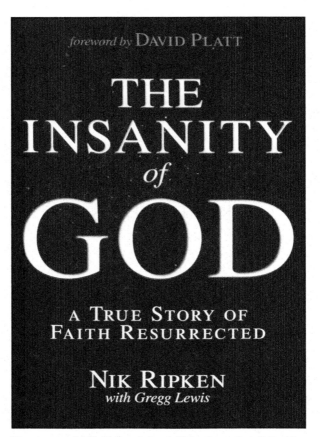

foreword by DAVID PLATT

THE INSANITY *of* GOD

A TRUE STORY OF FAITH RESURRECTED

NIK RIPKEN
with Gregg Lewis

The cover of Nik Ripken's book "The Insanity of God," a bestseller. The Ripken family leaned on Tim and Pam during some tragic times.

———— FOREWORD ————

BY NIK RIPKEN, AUTHOR OF
"THE INSANITY OF GOD"

I met Tim Maynard years before he had the word "Doctor" as a prefix to his name. We sat next to each other through doctoral classes at the Southern Baptist Theological Seminary in Louisville, Kentucky. He was pastor at the Bardstown Junction Baptist Church in Kentucky and we had just returned home from our first five years as missionaries in Malawi and South Africa. Thus, began a friendship that would deepen and grow over the next three decades as Tim and Pam, and their children, walked with us through the racism of apartheid, health issues resulting from continued bouts of malaria, and the tragedy that continues to be Somalia.

After immediate family, Tim and Pam were the first friends and church, that we called from Kenya when our 16-year-old son died on Easter Sunday morning from a severe asthma attack.

Tim and Pam kept our three boys and generated love gifts so that we could take vacations when we were on furlough in the States. They provided us with safe places to speak, rest, and be loved. They led their churches to send us gift boxes, almost monthly, those years they pastored in Kentucky. Once, I called Pam from Ethiopia to check on her after foot surgery. Immediately, she turned the conversation to our needs rather than focus on her own health concerns. After that phone call, she and Tim challenged the Sunday School classes at their new place of service, the Fruit Cove Baptist Church outside of Jacksonville, Florida to collect foodstuffs and treats that were totally unavailable, at that time, in Ethiopia. Shockingly, months later we received three wooden pallets, 4'x4' by 6' tall, packed with candy, chocolate bars, popcorn, Kool-Aid — more goodies than could be found in any store in Ethiopia (maybe in all of Africa!). This "gift" weighed more than 1,000 pounds with enough popcorn to fill the local airport along with enough Kool-Aid to flavor the Red Sea! It took two to three weeks to clear customs. We had to hire an import/ export specialists. Further, we had to ask Fruit Cove to help us pay the impressive import taxes, as the government had accused us of starting a completely stocked, unlicensed store, filled with international foods!

You've probably heard the phrase, "they loved us to death." Tim and Pam had this ability, and they could lead others in loving beyond all measure.

For more than 30 years Tim and Pam have served us overseas. Their churches have funded our projects and sent us volunteers. It provides a mission house that particularly serves missionaries from North Africa and the Middle East. At great expense, and some danger, Tim has led teams from their churches to meet us in secure locations, so that our teams from Somalia, Yemen, Ethiopia, Eritrea, and Djibouti could meet and worship together for the first time in three years. I will never forget observing missionaries, by the hundreds, weeping as the praise team from Fruit Cove Baptist Church led us in worship unlike we had been able to experience for the last three or more years.

One of the greatest joys, and greatest pains, of our lives has been this gift from God, that allows us to walk with Pam, Tim, their children, and the Fruit Cove community during this difficult season of Pam's illness and death, knowing that life must still be lived.

I have seldom, if ever, watched a family and community, while in such pain, walk with such tremendous faith. I have seldom, if ever, witnessed a husband, days after the home-going of his wife, stand before a congregation of thousands and "Bear Witness" to his growing love for his wife and her growing witness during those closing four months of her life.

Therefore, I bear witness that the funeral service of Pam Maynard was one of the top worship experiences of my life. I bear witness that the love of the Fruit Cove Baptist Church, and others within the faith community, exceeded almost all earthly expressions of God's love. I bear witness that during terrible crisis sometimes you just want someone to tell you the truth about God's nature alongside issues of life and death. Tim Maynard, being the brother that he is, has allowed me, his brother, access to the most tender places of his soul. I bear witness that during the darkest months, days, and hours of his life that Tim Maynard was, and is, like his Lord Jesus Christ.

He is trying his faith-filled best to bring resurrection out of crucifixion.

Often, when the truth and reality of death is ever present, the grace of the resurrection is seemingly deferred. Yet I bear witness that it is because of the pain of Pam's loss that grace was offered; offered by the church, offered by community, offered by a grieving family, and, most of all, offered by Dr. Tim Maynard.

Tim's family and the Ripken family have been on many journeys together. We have yelled on the Kentucky Wildcats. Tim and I have wondered at times who are these women that we married who can be so passionate about a basketball game? We have journeyed to the mountains of Ethiopia and the deserts of Dubai. He loved our boys and helped us walk through the death of one of them. We have loved his daughter and son along with his son-in-love and daughter-in-love. We are now walking through the death of all deaths, that of a spouse.

We will walk with the extended Maynard family and Fruit Cove community as we make sure that a little girl named McCail Violet will love, know, and own the story of her Mamaw. To this we bear witness, for her and for possible siblings and cousins yet to be born. They will keep her home filled with love and good food. They will envision her filling heaven with the soaring sounds of an organ being played to the delight of angels. They will scream with laughter as they watch videos of Mamaw playing the role of "Enamel." They might even go to yard sales as a memorial to the Queen of all yard sales! They will love Poppy, as she loved him. They will know and love Jesus, as she loved Jesus with all her heart.

Of these things...We.Bear.Witness.

We bear witness that Dr. Tim Maynard is "grieving well." He is doing so before his God, his family, those who call him pastor, and before a friend such as David had been for Jonathan. This book allows us the rarest of gifts. Tim courageously takes his lacerated heart and places it squarely in the hands of God and the community of faith. It is a rare gift, one to be treasured, and one from which to learn. It is the gift of faith in the resurrection even while the stone is still rolled in place.

Dr. Nik Ripken

Pam with her sweet McCail.

PREFACE:

DEAREST MCCAIL

I don't know how old you'll be when you see this. When the time is right, I'm sure. I want you to know that, although you were not quite a year and a half old when all of this came to pass, you had already made a tremendous impact on your Mamaw and Poppy.

Your Mamaw Pam loved you very much. I am writing this with tears flowing because I remember her making me promise that I wouldn't let you forget who she was and how much she loved you. I told her this: Every time your granddaughter looks into the mirror, she will see your eyes looking back at her!

Your visits, your pictures on the phone, and even your name lit up her eyes in the worst of her days. Whenever your Daddy or Momma planned a visit with us, no matter how hard it was for her, your Mamaw insisted that we get her dressed and her makeup on and help her to sit up because she didn't want you to remember her being sick and in a wheelchair.

Mamaw loved to do things with her hands. That was part of what made her sickness so hard for her. She couldn't hold you like she wanted, or make you pretty things. She wanted to teach you how to make cupcakes, and how to play with dolls. She wanted to take you for walks in Alpine Park and teach you how to recognize the names of flowers and plants which she knew and loved so well. We had even built a special garden spot out back called "Mamaw's Secret Garden" where she was already planning to spend pretty spring and summer days showing you how to plant and grow flowers!

You reminded us so much of your Daddy when he was little and being with you was like getting to be with your Daddy as a little boy all over again. Some of his younger pictures and yours are almost identical!

She wanted to be your "buddy," as well as your Mamaw. She had a little wagon out in the garage that she had planned to put you in and take you for walks. She wanted to spoil you with too many toys and too many nice clothes at Christmas and on your birthday.

You were the light of her life, as you are now of mine. She wanted you to learn to play piano like she did, and read you books and Bible stories. She had hoped to take you for manicures and pedicures and have "girl days" together.

But God had other plans for her and for us. We have had to learn to move on in life without her. I wanted you to have this book to read so you could know things about her and about me that people couldn't tell you.

Your Mamaw was a lady who was fun, and elegant, and

Tim, Pam and McCail are all smiles.

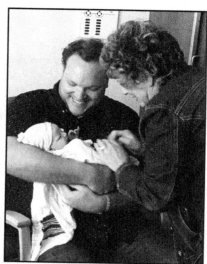

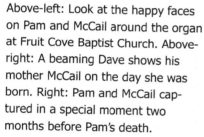

Above-left: Look at the happy faces on Pam and McCail around the organ at Fruit Cove Baptist Church. Above-right: A beaming Dave shows his mother McCail on the day she was born. Right: Pam and McCail captured in a special moment two months before Pam's death.

lovely, and kind, and who loved the Lord with all her heart. She wanted you to love the Lord too, and to love to go to church like she loved it. She wanted you to sing with a beautiful voice. Mamaw loved music so much! She wanted to teach you to love music, too. And she wanted to take you to yard sales and teach you how to find treasures in junk.

Maybe that is one of the things I loved most about your Mamaw; she could always find treasure in junk. A long time ago, way over forty years now, she met me when my life didn't have much of treasure to it. And she helped me find the "treasure" in my "junk."

People your Mamaw worked with as a nurse loved her for the same reason, I think. She so loved to help people get well. But the hardest and most broken people would be drawn to her because she could see more than the "junk" in their life. I don't think I realized that until she passed away. It was a gift God gave her that made her more like Him.

You are like her, McCail. You will always honor her anytime you take care of a lovely plant or smell a pretty flower. You will remember her any time you find treasure where other people only see junk. You will love her when you praise and use your voice to sing to Jesus.

One last thing. She always smelled so pretty! She loved to hug you and leave her beautiful fragrance on you. And as long as you live her fragrance will always be inside you.

Love, Poppy

Tim found only one partner who could dance
with him.

Tim and Pam share a nice moment.

INTRODUCTION

E very couple should have a song. A theme. Many do: A reminder of good times that cement their commitment...that celebrates their relationship. Pam and I have had a couple in our forty-plus years together.

Our first, and without a doubt, most enduring was a song written by a "Jesus music" pioneer named Michael Omartian. More people today would know him as the husband of Stormie, the author of dozens of books encouraging the prayer lives of women.

But when Michael and Stormie started out, they were a songwriting duo, he a musician and producer and she, the wordsmith of the team. Their first album, now obscure, was called "White Horse." It defined the sound of much of the LA-based Christian music taking the nation by storm in the 1970s.

On that first album, which played almost non-stop on the turntable in our first home, was a song entitled "Right From the Start." And right from the start, in the embryonic days of our marriage, we embraced that song as "our song" which defined our commitment and branded our marriage relationship.

The "hook" line in the refrain simply said, "Right from the start, it was right to the end." Through the years, those words appeared on our notes and cards written to each other, speaking our promise that no matter what, our love would endure "right to the end." This book is about what that looks like.

The path that life and God's Sovereign plan takes us has twists and turns that test us and can threaten to tear us apart. It is during those storms that it is easier to sing our commitment than to speak it. During the difficult days, the music needs to soar above the pain and beyond the trial. I heard it said somewhere that marriage is simply the act of one person bearing witness to the life of another. It is not a momentary accomplishment, but a lifetime of little acts, courageous decisions, selfless service and sacrificial love. We bear witness to each other as life is lived out.

One of the last words I spoke to Pam before her death was "right from the start, it was right to the end." Though she was unconscious as I said it, I still believe she heard it...and hopefully in her soul, sung it back to me. We bore witness to each other's lives and sang a song of committed love to each other as we did so...a life and a song I pray was pleasing to our God and Savior.

Underlying the story you will read in the pages to follow is that song. It weaves in and out of every sentence—a melody that kept us focused on the Lord as well as each other. A song that began from our earliest days of our learning and growing and understanding each other as we began the journey of becoming soulmates. And a psalm that carried us through the darkest and most difficult trial of our lives as we learned about each other and loss...and the goodness and grace of God.

Right from the start. And right to the end.

PART 1

BEGINNINGS

Pam as a beautiful senior at Catlettsburg High School.

I TAKE THEE, PAM,
TO BE MY WIFE

I can't dance. I admit it. There are witnesses, so denial isn't possible. I dance like a three-legged rhinoceros with gout. It's a family trait, inherited from my father and passed on to me and my brother. But then, we're Baptists. SOUTHERN Baptists. And you know what they say about Baptists and dancing: "Some can, and some can't." I can't.

When I was still struggling along in the seventh grade, trying to find my stride and my place in the world, my mother and some other well- intentioned moms decided it would be a good thing for their awkward sons to take some dance lessons and enter a middle school talent show at Coles Junior High in Ashland, Kentucky. How they convinced us this was OK I'll never know (Moms can be persuasive), but I painfully remember taking lessons at the June Conn Dance Studio in Ashland. Mrs. Conn was teaching us a classic top hat and cane routine. It was just as bad as you might imagine with four clumsy middle school boys using canes and wearing sequined coats and hats. Let's just say it did not further our effort to find our place in the world...or maybe it did, but it was not a place we cared to occupy.

As a side note, the June Conn School of Dance is now a shooting range in my hometown. Apparently her doomed attempt to teach me caused her to quit teaching dance. Guess we'll never know. And, if pictures of that ill-fated effort still exist, I will make certain nobody ever sees them!

So I couldn't dance. It had been scientifically proven. But I've learned that dancing is not a solo act. Dancing requires the right partner. Two lives, two souls, two bodies moving together as one. A good partner can overcome the limitations of the other.

That was us. Pam was my wife, my partner in life and ministry, and my best friend for over forty years. She could dance. She made me look really, really good. Sadly, not always on the dance floor, though I did learn to do a mean box step to our favorite romantic "dance" song, the Righteous Brothers "Unchained Melody." We could cut a mean rug at wedding receptions, and I usually did not embarrass her or step on her feet!

I have often in counseling and preaching stated that soulmates are not born, they are made. It takes a lifetime. We sometimes mistakenly assume that there is that "perfect someone" out there for us just "waiting" to be found and, in the moment it happens, birds sing, and rainbows appear, and the sky turns sunny and blue.

And so we search; online, dating sites, meet-and-greets, getting set up by your good friends... always looking for that serendipity that says "THIS IS THE ONE." Sadly some believe they did not marry their soulmate, so they violate their wedding vows and dump them for one who requires less effort. One marriage expert said that we have a decision to make when we get married. We will either try to be married to the fantasy, or be married to the reality. Sadly we sometimes tear up the reality trying to make it into a fantasy. We need to tear up the fantasy, and accept the real person God has brought to us.

But in the deepest sense the word can be used, on every dimension, Pam was my soulmate. It did not begin that way. We had to learn the dance. We had to suffer through awkwardness, and toes being stepped on, and one of us being out of step with the other. Life as a married soul is a life of continual adjustments... some microscopic, and some much larger. It is, sometimes beautifully...artfully...and sometimes awkwardly, a dance of two souls becoming one in every way possible.

Pamela Sloas was a different person than I, and yet our backgrounds and upbringing were very similar.

Our parents worked for the same place: the Ashland Oil Refinery. We attended and were baptized in the same church, located just half a block down from her home on Oakland Avenue in the small town of Catlettsburg, Kentucky. I grew up less than ten miles away and a jog to the north in the larger city of Ashland.

We were different. She was outgoing, gregarious, and the person everyone wanted to be around. If Facebook had existed in the seventies, she would have had friends numbering in the thousands. She was joyful and aware of the world around her, and had a childlikeness about her that she never lost.

Pam was the "girl next door," I guess we could say. And we did say. She had charisma that drew people to her. She was witty, and the joker of the crowd, a trait our son would later inherit. In

Pam was always cheering others on, even the Wildcats during her high school days at Catlettsburg High School.

her junior year, she was the Homecoming Queen of her high school. She liked to join things—school clubs, student council—and I'm sure if they had one, she would have joined the Chess Club.

And did she ever love to cheer! Her high school years were filled with lots of losses in football and basketball, but she was the captain of the high school cheering squad. And, although I only had the opportunity once to see her in action, she was the most enthusiastic cheerleader on the team and, in my opinion, the cutest!

She and I did not intersect much in those years. We ran in different circles, despite things we had in common. Life seemed

Pam with her family: father Leonard, mother Shirley and sisters Tracey (front) and Debbie (back right) in much earlier days.

to be bent on sending us in opposite directions.

Pam also liked belonging, and as a child it bothered her deeply to know her family was going to go to Heaven without her if she didn't give her heart to Jesus. So at eleven years of age, she walked forward in Vacation Bible School and gave her heart to Jesus. And she never looked back.

Once she was on your team, Pam had your back. She was fiercely loyal...to her family, her friends, her faith, her country... and later to me. She decided fairly early in her high school years that she was going to be a nurse and she spent forty years of her life serving people as a surgical nurse in five different hospitals. She never looked back...and never regretted the decision.

Again, she and I were different people. It was what made our dance unique. It was what kept us moving together, striving for the oneness that God had designed for us. It was what brought my life such joy.

It was how we became soulmates.

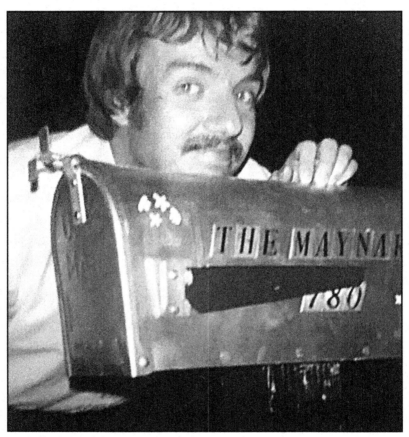

Tim was proud of his first mailbox.

I TAKE THEE, TIM, TO BE MY HUSBAND

They say opposites attract. Again, I believe this to be true. It is not our similarities that keep us together...but our dissimilarities...our differences that bring chemistry and romance and sticking power to the equation.

When Adam and Eve, the first man and woman, came together the Book of Genesis said that Eve was a person who "complemented" Adam in every way. That meant where Adam had weaknesses, Eve had strengths and where Eve had weaknesses, Adam had strengths. But the "gaps" between their strengths and weaknesses were what united them as one. I sincerely believe that if two people are exactly the same, one of them is unnecessary! We do not hold hands by matching fingers together, but by our fingers "filling the gaps" in the other person's hands. The differences create the dynamic...and the durability. In fact, the Hebrew Old Testament uses the same word to describe how Adam and Eve related and how people hold hands...by filling gaps!

Our backgrounds, while similar in many ways, had marked differences. One of those ways was in our parent's orientation toward life. Her parents were salt-of-the-earth people who believed in and lived a strong work ethic. Her mother, Shirley, was a hard-working homemaker, who made her daughter's clothing and was an award-winning quilter.

Her father, Leonard, would spend much of his time off from driving a transport truck for Ashland Oil tending his personal garden in his yard at home or at his mother's family farm across the river in nearby Ohio. They worked hard, saved their money, and lived a simple but joyful life. She grew up with her older sister Debbie and later, a younger sister named Tracey came along...fourteen years after Pam!

My parents, Clarence and Peggy Maynard, both worked hard, and provided us with a successful, happy, middle-class home life. My mom worked much of our childhood outside of the home as a receptionist for Ashland Oil Refinery. We lived on a nice street, in a lovely home, in a nice, safe part of town. But both of my parents had come from families different from Pam's parents, and my parents both rose above difficult backgrounds and succeeded in life. They raised my brother Mark and me in a much better world than they knew as children.

Family was significant to Pam's folks, and they had a large tight-knit family that would meet annually for reunions on her mother's side, and kept up with each other. To miss the Roberts family reunion in July was a capital offense, in their opinion!

My parents, on the other hand, came from families that left

them carrying some baggage. We did not grow up having reunions on my mom or my dad's side, though I do have some great holiday memories with a few members of both sides of the family tree. There were some members of the family that we kept up with, but not nearly like Pam's family did.

Pam was usually the "belle of the ball," while I was more of the retiring loner who kept to myself. I look at some of my high school pictures today, and realized I never really looked happy. I don't remember being unhappy...just intense. I do not have one picture of me in our high school yearbooks in which I was smiling. Not one! But Pam was laughing in all of hers.

The world was simpler to her...you were either doing right or doing wrong. For me, life was gray and sometimes fuzzy around the edges. I could see things from a different perspective. I was more serious, it seemed. She would make a judgement about a person or an idea quickly...and then not let it go. I would take too much time thinking through the options, and sometimes never make a decision.

I wanted to blend into the woodwork. As a musician, I "blended in" with my group...the high school band. We marched 160 members, plenty of uniforms to get lost in. She was the Homecoming Queen and cheerleader...hardly one to hide out! She was an extrovert; I was an introvert. She knew everyone. I could count my friends on one hand with a finger left over.

As did Pam, I also gave my heart to Jesus as a child. A nine-year-old, I marched down the same church aisle she did. I was baptized in the same baptistry. But her baptism seemed to take, while mine didn't. Her childhood commitment to church was deeper than mine early on.

I rebelled later and went off the rails when I was sixteen. A sullen teenager who was sneaking cigarettes and sampling alcohol and listening incessantly to rock music, I became a difficult child to my parents. The extent of her rebellion was staying out sometimes past curfew. I started playing drums in local nightclubs in nearby Ohio when I was seventeen, and got in because I looked older than my age. I seldom came home before four in the morning. To my knowledge, Pam never saw the inside of a bar...at least not the kind I played in.

In my later teen years, I began to play seven nights a week in a local bar, and then eventually began to travel with a club band. It was during those early years of wandering that I took a side job in a band with a professional clown known simply as "Coco the Clown." A Polish Jew by nationality and religion, he had retired from Ringling Brothers, Barnum and Bailey Circus and moved to our part of Kentucky to raise pigs. He offered to take our band on the road with him to do events at elementary schools, dressed as clowns. He called it "Coco's Clown College." At night, we would "adult" up the routines a bit and perform our musical clown show at local nightclubs. I wanted to play drums and get paid for it, so I agreed to this...and wore the greasepaint. So my pattern of traveling, coupled with an unsupervised, out-of-control lifestyle continued as we toured in New York State and other places north.

This unhealthy cycle continued until I was twenty, and after yet another band crashed and burned, I was broke and needed to move back home. I had been to the far country for the previous four years, and was tired of living with the pigs. My dad said I could live at home if I would give up traveling, and if I agreed to

Tim and Pam were some cool cats in the 1970s.

go to vocational school to "learn a trade." I did. It was a fateful decision, and my path toward a spiritual return as well as my intersection with Pam had begun.

Hope was about to crash into my life!

Pam's senior photo from Catlettsburg High School.

OPPOSITES ATTRACTING

The opposite poles of a magnet do indeed attract, as do the opposite polarities of electron charges. Our Creator designed nature to be such, and these opposing differences are actually some of the properties that attract and hold things together. Sometimes marriages are abandoned because of "irreconcilable differences." My contention is that, without those differences, nobody would stay together for long. The process of those differences bumping against each other creates the formula and energy and chemistry in which soulmates are formed.

My first real glimpse of Pam, the girl next door, came in the hallway of Ashland Community College. I saw this vision at a distance...the girl of my dreams...dressed in platform shoes, blue jeans, and a furry short coat. Her eyes, her hairstyle...well, everything...caught my attention and my breath. She was everything I had dreamed of in a girl! A little bit of a hippie, but classy at the same time.

I put on the coolest look and walk I could muster (remembering back, I must have been trying to look like John Travolta strutting in Saturday Night Fever, the top of my shirt strategically opened) and approached this beautiful creature to get a closer look. It was then I realized it was Pam Sloas! The cheerleader! The Homecoming Queen! And as I got closer, she was smiling and waving as she saw me....ME! If I remember correctly, that was the first time she ever accelerated my heart rate...but it would not be the last.

We went to the lounge and chatted for a few minutes, catching up on the past few years, and I then mustered my courage and asked her if she was seeing anyone. She said she was, so I said (to myself) "That's it for me." I'm sure I must have said something real cool to her, and then walked away (again, cue the BeeGees singing "Stayin' Alive").

One of our big differences was in the areas of confidence and the love of competition. I had little of one and none of the other. The June Conn School of Dance had beaten what little confidence I had out of me! She had lots...of both. I assumed I would be rejected, so I left our brief encounter guessing that was so and decided then and there I wouldn't try to compete for her affections. How could I? After all, what did I have to offer the Homecoming Queen?

But she didn't leave my mind. Her voice, her perfume, her eyes, how she looked haunted me. I was not looking for a girlfriend or trying to fall in love, but every love song I heard from then on caused my mind to drift to thoughts about her. Borrowing a phrase from a song popular at that time, I had "fooled around and fell in love." This girl did it for me!

I started going back to church (one of my father's conditions for free room and board), but now I realized this might actually work well for me. Pam went there, too. She played the organ! Each Sunday I would sit strategically near her so she could see I was there. I complimented her playing...casually of course (though my heart now beat out of my chest when I got close to her...kept thinking of that first meeting), and after church I would sit in the parking lot waiting for my Dad to wrap up his duties as Minister of Music.

I parked our bright orange 1974 VW Beetle strategically to see Pam as she walked the short distance to her house...usually surrounded by a gaggle of boys. But as she walked past, I would wave nonchalantly while singing Joe Cocker's "You Are So Beautiful" to her through the VW's windshield. And if you're wondering, I sang as well as I danced. Best the windows were left rolled up!

Now my father was a smart man, and perceptive. He liked Pam and her family...a lot. He had already decided, old school, that one of his sons was going to marry her...he didn't care if it was me or my brother Mark. So when he noticed my infatuation with her, he decided to help his shy prodigal son out. Soon he began to conspire with her mother to make this happen.

An event happened in June of which my dad was in charge. He needed a pianist to accompany some singing at a local retreat center. Pam agreed to go and play for him, but needed a ride. Dad agreed to pick her up, and then at the last minute had an "errand" to run, and asked me to go get her instead. "It'll really help me out," he lied.

Left: Pam was always gorgeous and elegant along with her sweet personality. Right: Pam, far right, was the Homecoming Queen during her senior year in high school.

I reluctantly and obediently complied...(right). In reality, I was jumping up and down inside, not letting my dad see what an incredible thing this was going to be for me. He knew it, but I think he wanted to see what I would do.

It took me two hours to get ready that day. I put on my coolest flared jeans, and a brand new polyester shirt, strategically opened to let some chest hair peek over (OK, it was cool then). I then immersed myself in (far, far too much) Jovan Musk cologne. The advertisement for the cologne said it was "an exotic blend of spices and woods combined with the seductive power of musk." Added to that recommendation, Dad already had some available in his bathroom! All I had was Old Spice.

I pulled up to her house at Oakland Avenue in my newly washed, recently repainted purple 1967 Ford Falcon, with my Musk wafting. She stood waiting on the porch, and I knew my moment had arrived at last. I politely opened the door for her, as she slid in with her bowl of warmed up peas leftover from lunch (which, though I did not care for peas, I ate eagerly at the dinner)!

And then, I had almost thirty glorious minutes in my car, alone with the girl who had stolen my heart but who didn't even know it yet; seeing her, hearing her talk and laugh, enjoying her fragrance. Surprisingly, my Musk had not destroyed my ability to smell.

Later, as things got boring at the event we were attending, I asked her to go for a walk with me. We immediately landed in a deep conversation about life, what we wanted to do with our lives (as if I knew...I just knew I wanted her). And then, something took over. Maybe my dad's prayer was being answered...I don't know. But filled with a surge of confidence, I asked her how serious she was with her current boyfriend, and if she would be interested in dumping him and going out on a date with me. I surprised her with that question...but surprised myself even more that I'd mustered the courage to ask it!

I invited her to go with me to get a lemonade at a nearby Dairy Cheer on the way back, (still had an hour or two left on the Musk), and we continued to talk about the guy she was "pre-" engaged to (he had given her a promise ring). Quickly I discerned that she had decided she didn't really want to be with him, but didn't know how to break up. "But," she quickly added, "if I break up with him, I need you to know I'm not looking for a quick fling. I'm ready for a serious boyfriend."

Pam with her sisters Debbie Vincini, left, and Tracey Harr.

By now, we had made our way back to her house and were standing in her front yard as the darkness of the evening fell and stars shone overhead. I said, "I'm looking for something serious, too. It won't be a casual relationship for me." And with that, I leaned over...and kissed her.

Then, for the third time surprising myself, I said the right thing: not sounding nearly as desperate or tongue-tied as I felt. "I'll give you some time. Think it over." And then, I walked away...no longer like John Travolta...more like Clint Eastwood... minus the cowboy hat.

I drove home singing "One of These Nights" with the Eagles; my arm stretched across the front seat of the Falcon, pretending she was still there...and kicking myself for not having had the nerve to do that when she was actually in the car! I promised myself that wouldn't happen again.

FIGHT NIGHT

Several days after our first romantic encounter, the Fourth of July holiday rolled around. Pam still hadn't spoken to her boyfriend (I learned later she was afraid...and why). She got word to me that her family was camping at nearby Carter Caves State Park and invited me to drop by.

I didn't even tell my parents goodbye. The car was flying out of the driveway in a purple blur and I was off! By the time I arrived, her family had gone to a lake to swim and, though I didn't own a swimsuit, I had brought scissors to cut off the blue jeans I was wearing so I could join them for a swim on the beach. It was a wonderful time!

And then it came ... "the voice" from above. Not God...but the voice of her angry boyfriend shouting down to her in the water from an overlook above. (Think of the first appearance of Darth Vader in Star Wars). He continued shouting her name until her mother made her go to him and calm him down.

From the beach, I glared up at him and watched carefully

with my best Clint Eastwood squint, hands on my hips to make my one hundred-and-sixty-five pound frame look larger and more intimidating as she approached him. They talked for a few moments, and then she came back down with the joyful news I had hoped to hear: she had broken up with him!

He planned later to come by her house so she could return his ring. I had gone on to work. Later that evening, he arrived at her house, demanding to know who I was and why she wanted to dump him for me. He then pushed her in anger and she fell to the ground as he stalked away, vowing to find me.

And he did. About one o'clock in the morning. I don't know how he learned where I lived, but all six-foot-three of him stood on my front porch, shouting for me to come out so he could teach me a lesson. "Darth" was not going to be pacified by simple explanations.

I was asleep in my bedroom with the window open, and heard him ranting outside. I got up, pulled on my jeans, and went outside barefoot and shirtless. Now dear reader, if I did anything worse than dancing, it was fighting. I had strategically avoided several in my lifetime, but this confrontation looked like it was going to end up in a brawl. In my driveway. In my nice neighborhood. At 1:00 a.m.

I tried to look as intimidating as I could (again, think Clint Eastwood), and asked what he thought he was doing. He said, "I've come here to warn you to stay away from my girl." I replied, "I have no intention of doing that. She doesn't want to date you" and with that, he shoved me backwards into our garage door.

When he did this, things went a little blurry and I thought, for the first time in my life, "I've got to hit this guy somewhere.

Hard." And it was then the grace of God appeared, because had I hit him he would probably have killed me!

My little brother Mark pulled up in his small Chevrolet, and like a clown car in the circus, six or seven of his posse...a couple of them big guys...crawled out of the car behind him. They just kept coming! They all "lived" in our basement, playing Strat-O-Matic baseball nonstop. As Mark's entourage walked up the driveway on their way to their basement hideout, they paused and each said, "How ya doing, Tim?" Mark told me later they thought "Darth" was just a friend of mine!

With that display of force, as he was apparently doing the math when they gathered around, my nemesis looked down at me and said, "Well, I'm not going to fight your whole gang!" And then he stalked away threatening, "Stay away from my girl!"

I didn't. And I never saw him again.

Whew!

Pam on Homecoming night with her proud father Leonard.

ROMANCE AND THE STONE

I had never dated before. Not seriously. Now, I had a real girlfriend who expected me to take her out on dates and spend money on her...and more than once! I wasn't really sure how to do that. I knew I wanted to be with her more than anything, so many dates we would go to a local park or get lemonade and just talk (well OK...we kissed a little too). Both of us were working at that time.

Often our dates would happen on the weekend, and we were so tired we would just fall asleep lying on opposite ends of her living room sofa with the TV blaring. Her mom thought it was cute. Her dad...well, let's just say he didn't like the idea of a young man in his house past eleven. I had learned to cleverly sneak out the front door when I saw his car lights coming in the driveway so I wouldn't have to face him as he entered the back door. But occasionally sleep won out, and I would find myself being awakened by her less-than-pleased father asking me, "Would you like to borrow some pajamas?"

I always hated leaving Pam. We would often talk of how nice it would be one day if we never had to leave each other again. That thought stuck with me...what if we never had to say goodnight and be apart? What if we could be together? Always? I was ready! Even after forty years of marriage, we hated being separated for long.

Life was about to change for us. Pam had already been accepted into the nursing program at Morehead State University, a dream of hers. But I couldn't let her go there without showing how serious I was about her. And we were about to enter the uncharted territory of a long-distance relationship-without cell phones or FaceTime!

I had stopped playing in nightclubs by then and was working in a service station full time. I was actually one of America's last "gas jockeys!" Money was scarce for me. It took a week for me to make the money I made in two nights playing clubs. But I knew I had to get a ring to ask her to marry me, and then ask her dad's permission. I was scared...of him, of what I was about to jump into...that he might say no...that she might say no! But I knew now was the time to ask.

Her father Leonard Sloas was not a large man. I was taller, and outweighed him. But he had taken time, as I dated his daughter, to thoughtfully and purposefully show me his guns, and his knife collection. He also had medals for being a sharpshooter in the military. He was a truck driver and those guys knew how to take care of themselves. He worked hard, was respected and respected those who also worked for a living. And I both respected him as a man who had "fought Hitler" (as he would tell you) in World War II, and certainly as a man who loved and cared for his family.

I, on the other hand, was a reconditioned hippie who had shown up on dates more than once in platform shoes (It was the seventies)! I dressed to impress Pam, not him. And I'm fairly certain I didn't impress him—at least not at first. He tolerated me because he knew my parents. I worked pumping the gas he delivered in his tanker. I worked for minimum wage, while he made some good money driving.

Naturally, he wanted to know what I planned to do to provide for us. "You can't keep working at a service station." I told him (translate that "made up") my career plans to work in the broadcast electronics field, and assured him there was "big money" there. He asked me "Will you be good to her...and always love her and try to make her happy?" I knew I was getting closer to "closing" the deal, so I eagerly said, "Sir, I give you my word." "Alright," he replied. "You take care of her." "I will sir," I said with my heart in my throat. And with that, he gave me his blessing!

I had scraped what little money I could together, went to a jeweler and bought a ring (which, upon reflection, should have come with its own magnifying glass so you could find the diamond), and, in the front seat of my purple Ford Falcon asked her to marry me.

OK, let's stop here for a moment. I know that a cheesy, microscopic diamond ring and a fabric seat in a '67 Ford is not romantic. There were no horse or canoe rides. No swan releases, rented islands, or airplanes skywriting "I love you" in the air. No waiter bringing an elegant dessert on cue, with a three- carat ring hidden inside. The floorboard of my car was not even covered in flower pedals, which in hindsight would have been romantic had I been able to afford them.

Just two people in love. Madly. Crazy about each other. I couldn't bear to leave her. She felt the same. I was honored that she would love someone like me. Uncreative in my asking, but sincere to the core of my soul, I asked, "Would you be my wife?"

She wept when I asked her. She said "yes." We kissed. That was it. I said, "I wanted you to know how serious I am before you leave for school." She said, "I am too." And that was enough.

For both of us.

COME TO JESUS

I t was now the mid-seventies. On the West Coast of the US mainland, a movement had begun at a church in Costa Mesa, California that changed the complexion of Christianity in America. The Jesus Movement had begun. Music was changing drastically...young people were re-engaging with the church. The hippies were abandoning Eastern mysticism and embracing the ancient Christian faith in mass numbers, and we got swept up in it.

In that era when Bill Gaither was still considered to be "of the devil" by some churches because he sang such devious songs as "Because He Lives," we began traveling in a Christian band playing some of this newfound, rock-and-roll Jesus music. A few other musicians, Pam and myself made up our band of gypsies... six in all with a sound man. A couple of the guys were as rough in their backgrounds as I had been. Our early dating and engagement months were filled with weekend outings playing music in churches and coffee houses and colleges throughout several states, traveling in a van or motor home. We would

Fun-loving Tim and Pam squeezed their way into a photo box designed for one.

sometimes deliver Pam to her dorm at Morehead State University at 3:00 or 4:00 on Monday morning, and she had classes starting at 7:30!

Although I traveled with a Christian group and played drums, I began having serious doubts about my own faith. I had, in fact, come under deep conviction that my faith was not authentic. I had begun to struggle some months before, and questioned the sincerity and validity of my childhood decision.

I confessed this reluctantly to Pam in the basement of my parent's house on December 26, 1975. She said, "Let's go see Bill" (our youth leader and singer for the band). Bill Traylor was cooler and older and wiser than we. He was 27 and married, and he owned a cherry red Corvette Stingray. When we knocked on his

Some early days of Tim and Pam's relationship.

door just before midnight, he opened and welcomed us in with a deeply concerned look. Sitting on his sofa in the living room, I confessed my uncertainty and questions about my faith to him. He led me to Scriptures that convinced me that I needed to repent and turn fully to trust in Christ alone...something I wasn't sure I had ever done.

That night I did so gladly, kneeling there on the green carpet of his living room floor. It was a chilly December evening in Kentucky. Christmas lights still shone brightly in the homes we passed as we drove to his house.

Bill lived at the top of what was tongue-in- cheek referred to as "holy hill" because the pastor of our church lived directly across the street from him. I still drive by this "holy place" when I'm back home, and just around the corner is the cemetery where my father is buried. It was appropriate that night as we ascended "the hill of the Lord" to settle this matter once and for all!

Honestly I wanted this so badly I would have stood on one leg and sung "Amazing Grace" if that's what I was supposed to do! God had reached deep into some dark places in my life and brought conviction of sin like I had never before known. Things that I had begun to tolerate and the lifestyle I had pursued so casually were suddenly causes of remorse and were now repulsive to me. As the Psalmist said, "I despise myself." I was ready for a new beginning...a return to the faith in which I had been raised. An embracing of that faith for myself, and not just because I had grown up in it.

Bill led me in a prayer that was written on the back of a paper evangelistic booklet produced by Campus Crusade for Christ. From it, he instructed me that I was to confess Jesus as Lord and turn from my sins, and trust in the atoning death and resurrection of Jesus Christ alone for my salvation. I was glad to do so, although I would still have to say, as best as I remember that moment, I wasn't sure what some of those words meant. But when I got up, my life was honestly never the same.

There were no fireworks or emotional excesses or flood of tears flowing. I had simply and sincerely decided to follow Jesus...no turning back. No turning back. This experience, for me, brought to life the Scripture that "if any man will open the door to Me I will come in..." I often remember back to that cold December night when a believer opened the door of his home, and then of eternal life to me.

And Pam was right there beside me when that happened.

JESUS PEOPLE

So I became a Jesus freak. A certified Bible thumper. A Bible "fanatic." The night of my conversion experience I came home after visiting a couple of friends to tell them what I had done (again, it was the middle of the night), and was so excited that I remained awake and read the Bible for the first time in my life with understanding. I could not get enough. I was like a starving man at the all-you-can-eat buffet! But for me, all you could eat was never enough. I wanted more.

So I was all in. I put a bumper sticker on my Falcon that warned, "Get Right or Get Left." On the other side of my bumper was a sticker that stated, "Heaven or Hell, make your choice." I was such a Jesus freak that I would ask a total stranger on the street if they knew whether or not they were going to heaven when they died. I passed out newspapers produced by Jesus People USA at rock concerts to those waiting in line outside.

I actually had a desire to go back into the bars where I had played to witness to the people I'd met there. Bill wisely counseled against that, convincing me I wasn't ready yet to face

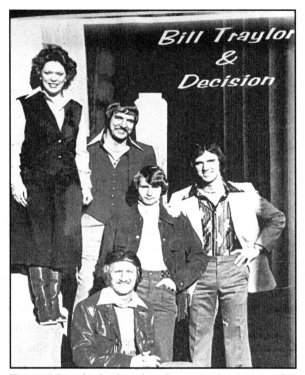

Tim and Pam both played in the group Decision and it was group leader Bill Traylor who led Tim to Christ.

that temptation. But I believed Jesus was coming back tomorrow, if not today. And I wanted to be ready! I even sold my most precious possession—a record collection (an "idol" in my life, I judged) and listened exclusively to the new Jesus music (and Jimmy Swaggert...don't ask why).

My mind and life were being made new. I was, in fact, a new creation in Christ and this time it was for real! While studying the Book of Revelation with a friend, I mastered the material in an ominous and imaginative book called "666" and Hal Lindsey's "The Late Great Planet Earth" (required reading for the serious Christian in the 70's). I had been to the edge once in my life, and I had no desire to go back there ever again.

During this season, Bill began to ask me to give my testimony at the end of our concerts. I had never done any public speaking, except for college speech class in which I had gotten a "C." But Bill owned me now. He had led me to Christ, had helped me leave the club life, and he was now discipling me. It was my turn to stand up and speak out for Jesus and prove that I was not ashamed of the Gospel or the Savior who died for me!

And so I shared. It took over fifteen minutes the first time I did it. I learned quickly that I could go to gusts of thirty minutes if so required! The first time I gave my testimony in public, my college speech teacher was present. As though to intimidate me, he leaned out into the aisle. I found out later he was just shocked to see me on the platform! Bill then started using me every time we played.

One weekend, we were told after arriving for a three-day retreat that we needed someone to speak on Sunday morning. He told them, "No problem." Then he turned to me and said, "Oh Tim, by the way..."

That Sunday morning, in the South Charleston Baptist Church in Charleston, West Virginia, I preached my first "sermon." Actually, it was a longer version of my testimony, with more Bible thrown in. Two women came up to me at different times after the service and said, "You know that God is calling you to preach?" The first time, I kind of laughed it off. Yeah right. The second time, I wasn't laughing. I got scared.

And I never forgot that weekend...or that moment.

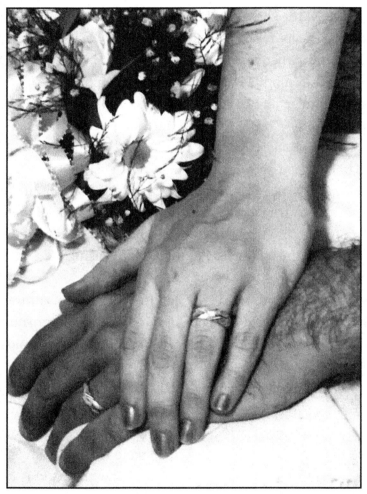

The hands of lovebirds on their wedding day.

PART 2

HAPPILY EVER AFTER

Wedding day on May 14, 1977 in Catlettsburg in the side lot of Oakland Avenue Baptist Church.

TO HAVE AND TO HOLD FROM THIS DAY FORWARD

P am and I wed on May 14, 1977. In the side yard of the Oakland Avenue Baptist Church, a garden spot at the time, we created an outdoor sanctuary. It was fitting for our day. It was fitting for Pam, surrounded as we were by flowering shrubbery and natural beauty. She always loved flowers. She wore a floral wreath in her hair. So we were married the day after she graduated with her nursing degree from Morehead State University.

I didn't learn until later that she had taken time out the week before and walked through a field of wildflowers, thinking about the commitment she was about to make. I never got the courage to ask what she had to think about...was my background too rough for her? Did she wish she were marrying "Darth" after all...or another old boyfriend? I won't ever get an answer to that question because I never found the courage to ask, but I'm so glad she showed up on our wedding day!

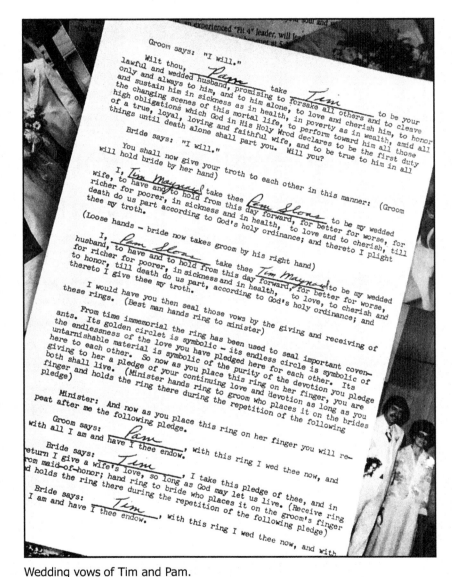

Wedding vows of Tim and Pam.

Our honeymoon was short and occurred in a less than romantic setting (sensing a theme here, are we)? We left our reception early and went to the Stone Lodge in Barboursville, West Virginia. It was, sadly, a dump. (It looked good on the billboard). There we spent our first night together as husband and wife. We both had to go back to work Monday, and we were taking the following long weekend to play a date with Bill Traylor and Decision in Myrtle Beach. We had actually bumped our wedding date back a week so we could be married when we went on that trip. Since we were the only couple in the condo rented for the weekend, the other four guys in the band graciously gave us the "honeymoon suite."

It was the first of many, many lessons we would learn that commitment to ministry was a mixed bag. It would involve inconveniences, sacrifices and difficulties for us as well as provide many joyful moments and opportunities. In those times there was always better...but sometimes there could be worse.

God had begun to teach us even then.

Tim and Pam at Bardstown Baptist Church in Kentucky where they served prior to coming to Fruit Cove Baptist Church in Florida.

THE CALLING

O ur first year as husband and wife was wonderful, though odd. We bought a 72-foot-long mobile home to live in and had planned to move it to a nearby rental lot. But we found, due to logistics in relocating it that we could not overcome, we had to stay. Nobody would move it! So with the permission of the new homeowners beside us, we stayed.

On the left side of our lot were our reluctant landlords...a young family with small children and two dogs who had just moved on the property themselves. The dogs quickly adopted us when they tasted the table scraps from Pam's meals! Once I accidentally pinned one of their dogs in under our trailer when I was working to winterize it. "Jerry" was there in the darkness for two days before anyone knew! He never barked once.

On our right sat a barn full of chickens. The chickens never adopted us, and squawked and clucked at all hours. We assumed a busy rooster must live there! At the top of a hill directly in front of us was a cemetery, which we tried not to think about. Our back

Pam always looked elegant and had the most beautiful home around.

Tim and Pam at Oakland Avenue Baptist Church with his brother Mark and wife Beth and his mother and father, Peggy and Clarence. Pam is holding Allison. It was 1982.

door led to a sheer drop of five or six feet that overlooked a 45 degree angle down a hillside. The mattress in our master bedroom was literally a piece of foam rubber that folded when we laid on it. But do you understand when I say that this was paradise on earth for us? A million dollar mansion would not have made us any happier!

Pam worked second shift at King's Daughter's Hospital in Ashland...the hospital where we were both born and where I had given my tonsils as a child in exchange for unlimited ice cream. She had begun in earnest working out her calling as a registered nurse. I, meanwhile, worked as a representative in customer service (aka, "the complaint department") for General Telephone, the local phone company. In a day of sixteen party telephone lines, I was busy with unhappy customers!

My job was to show up in a suit and sit in a small office and listen to people complain about their phone problems eight hours a day. Engaging stuff, but in hindsight it was good training for ministry! Pam and I were both happy to be gainfully employed, and truly enjoyed having our own money, paying our own bills, and making it on our own. We owned a little black-and-white TV set, complete with rabbit ears covered in aluminum foil, and listened constantly to Christian music.

During the long evenings while she worked, I began reading and building a library of Christian literature and read everything from Charles Spurgeon to Halley's Bible Handbook to, well, some really off- the -wall stuff. But I was learning to separate the wheat from the chaff, and those late evenings were my first seminary.

We were frozen out by the winter storms of 1977-78, and spent a month living in my parent's basement. But we survived...

though the plumbing in our trailer didn't. By the spring thaw, God had begun gnawing at my heart and my resistance to that troubling incident in Charleston, West Virginia a year before. I had concluded, reluctantly and with some fear, that God indeed was calling me ... us ... into the ministry.

So in March of our first year of marriage, I related my sense of call to her. The next day, a Sunday, we walked forward to share this with our church family. Pam looked shellshocked, because she was. Her life had just exploded! The church was elated. But this was not her plan, nor was it mine actually. I had more time to think it through than I gave her, and unfairly I expected her to follow without question or further discussion. She did, as Sarah followed Abraham. She often told pastor's wives in conferences in later years that God did not call her to be a pastor's wife. He called her to be my wife, and whatever I am that's who she is too.

And by faith, we set out on the journey that would define the rest of our lives. God was at work!

COLLEGE DAYS

By our first wedding anniversary, I had been offered a full scholarship to attend Cumberland College in Williamsburg, Kentucky. The scholarship involved playing drums in a newly formed ensemble that promoted the college by touring through the southeast and Ohio. Rehearsals were beginning soon, and the touring would begin later in the summer.

So we sold everything. Our trailer, our furniture, her washer and dryer, our second car, until all we owned barely filled half of a small U-Haul. We bid goodbye to our friends, and family, our adopted dogs, and the chickens. We wept as we shared a final meal of Giovanni's Pizza on the front porch stoop of our dream home, where we had shared many romantic and hasty "picnic" lunches in the past months together, and where God had truly begun the working of knitting two people into one.

In fairness to Pam, our telling of this part of the story would be different. For me, there was excitement, not only of playing music with a talented group of singers and musicians for Jesus,

Pam's alter-ego "Enamel," which entertained hundreds with down-home humor. She was talented in anything she did.

but even more the anticipation of studying and learning the Bible. I had developed a hunger to learn, and the limited resources available to me where we lived had begun to frustrate me, like eating fastfood when you really want a home-cooked meal.

Fast forward a bit with me. When Pam and I started leading marriage enrichment events a few years later in Louisville she adopted an "alternate personality," a tacky country girl named "Enamel (pronounced EEE-nuh-Mel) Carver, so named by her Daddy, who was a painter. He found her name on a paint can one day. Enamel was the queen of one-line zingers, and her make-believe husband Jeb was a taxidermist with a business whose motto was "The Buck Stops Here."

One of her favorite lines about her marriage to Jeb was that when they married it was for better or worse. She'd say, "Jeb couldn't have done much better...I couldn't have done much worse." In this instance, I'm sure she was thinking back on this move.

For her, (Pam...not Enamel) this move meant a loss of security, a separation from deep friendships and family connections, and adjustment to a new life in an apartment complex filled with strangers. Not only that, but a nightmarish job awaited her in a rural, mountain hospital on third shift.

She was now married to a full-time student without a job, and who was gone much of the time on the road. The sacrifices she made with little complaint are nothing short of remarkable, and God gave her great grace to endure this...and I believe great and eternal honor now for doing so. Let it be said that she paid the highest price for my decision.

We were not living in poverty in college, to be honest. Pam had a better job than most student wives, and we were able to afford an apartment off-campus. But our budget did not allow for vacations. It did allow for travel, say, to a free weekend in a vacation timeshare presentation. We went to a couple. I know, I know. That was really cheap and there was no way we would ever have afforded a timeshare. But we called it even since they solicited us. It only took us a few hours to attend the presentation, and we would just be out the cost of gas and a couple of meals while there. A bargain in any book. Plus we got to go to a few places we could never have afforded otherwise.

While at Cumberland College, I had a biology professor who was undoubtedly the most boring professor I had ever heard. Dr. Milton was older, and corny in his presentations and lame efforts at telling jokes. But when I served later as his assistant, I learned some things about him. He was truly brilliant, far more so than his presentations would convey. And he loved God passionately. His love for science and biology, far from tearing his faith down, reinforced it. He taught me that science and faith, in their truest forms, were not in conflict but should in fact be compatible if correctly understood.

In our second year in Williamsburg, our first medical crisis as a married couple occurred. Pam ended up needing surgery on a softball-sized cyst on her ovary. Though benign, it needed to be removed.

She underwent a three-hour procedure to have this growth extracted. It was the longest three hours I had ever experienced. And if I had undergone the procedure without anesthesia myself, it would not have hurt me more. I was learning even then that being one with a person is not only sharing emotion, but pain as well. I sat in stony, reflective silence in the waiting room, surrounded by caring professors, pastors, and friends from our college community.

Later that night, after the surgery was completed, I sat by her bedside, holding her hand and stroking her hair, in the twilight of the room. A quiet knock came at the door, and Dr Milton slipped into our room. He stayed for a few brief moments, blessed Pam with a prayer, and left us with a prophecy neither of us ever forgot.

He said, "I believe, no matter what happens in your lives, that you two are going to find a way to be happy together." He then left the room as quietly as he had entered.

And you know, even to the end, he was so right.

SEMINARY BOUND

As we wrapped up our time in college, a decision loomed. I had begun to shrink back a bit from the decision to go on to seminary. I realize now I was burnt out, having embraced school so eagerly and fervently. I graduated Magna Cum Laude, and was even honored with a college leadership award in 1980.

Part of what fed my reluctance was a recurring colon problem that had first struck when I was only fourteen. Ulcerative colitis had almost killed me then, and was threatening to try it again. The stress of school and decisions about the future fed the cycle that made me sicker.

Added to that stress was an opportunity to go to Nashville and pursue a full-time career, traveling and playing in Southern Gospel music. Though not the music of my choice, I had friends there and a connection that may possibly have allowed me to work with some popular groups touring in that day. And they would pay me to do what I loved! The temptation was tremendous, though doing this meant that Pam would once again

Tim and Pam at his graduation with a master's degree from
Southern Theological Seminary in Louisville.

be a "road widow," with a traveling musician for a husband. She deeply resisted me doing this, but my health, I believed, would not allow me to continue under the load of study and work at seminary.

One day as we were driving and discussing this decision, we came to an interstate sign that said LOUISVILLE-NASHVILLE. It seemed to capture our crossroad dilemma. Once again, she was allowing me to make the final decision, but she also let me know how she felt.

Later that day after a lengthy discussion, we decided to continue the application process at The Southern Baptist Theological Seminary in Louisville. She began immediately applying for work in several Louisville-area hospitals and quickly received a job offer to work at Norton Hospital. It was cutting edge, and a great place for her to work with world-renown spine and orthopedic surgeons.

We moved in the summer, after an August graduation from Cumberland College. I had stalled our decision too long for us to get seminary housing, so we moved to a nearby apartment. We both detested it. It was loud, smelled unpleasant, and separated us from the seminary community.

Three months later, we found a way to get onto campus in the newest apartment complex on Grinstead Drive in Louisville. The downside was it was a three-story complex and our home was going to be on the third floor. Up sixty-six stairs (yes, I counted). But it seemed like a wonderful dream come true, and was in fact an apartment that we had specifically sat outside in the parking lot, looked at, and asked God for. He put the desire in both of our hearts for that specific apartment. And then He gave it. We moved in gladly and gratefully.

Our first years at seminary were about as hard as I had feared. My illness had continued to spiral downward. My hemoglobin level dropped drastically, as did my weight (I had lost down to 165 pounds). With my full beard, ill-fitted clothing, and emaciated appearance, I looked like a refugee from Woodstock. And I was running on empty.

During this time, we also agreed to take a church in inner-city Louisville, at an intersection of the worst part of the city. Housing projects surrounded us, but so did opportunities to minister like we had never seen. Children and youth came to this aging church building and equally aging congregation. Many, who had never heard it before, came to hear about the love of God and the gift of salvation who had never heard it before. The children were mesmerized by Pam as she planned fun events for them on Wednesday nights.

Sunday morning she had begun playing an old organ with an air bellows that whooshed when she pressed the pedals. Dust would literally fly out of the speakers as she played!

Serving Immanuel Baptist Church was the hardest, and best ministry we could have had as a seminary couple. Our pastor unfortunately was a wounded man with a lot of baggage, so after two years of spiritual struggle under his leadership, we began to pray to go somewhere else.

Little did I know that this prayer would lead to our first pastorate.

—— PART 3 ——

BECOMING THE PASTOR'S FAMILY

Tim and Pam in their younger and, uh, much cooler days.

REVEREND AND
MRS. MAYNARD

I was never comfortable (and I'm still not) with "reverend" in my title. That said, that was what was what I was about to become! A small congregation thirty miles south of Louisville near Shepherdsville, Kentucky had asked me to come and fill their pulpit as a guest speaker. After the second visit, they asked if I would like to be considered as their next pastor. My biggest fear was that they would find out I only had two good sermons, and they had already heard them both!

They invited me to consider this opportunity in March of 1982. Had they asked me in February, I would have flatly told them no. Or maybe even an emphatic "no way." But by the second month of my spring semester, I had been sitting under the teaching of Dr. Findley Edge. His book, *Renewal in the Church*, had rocked my world. And one day in class, Dr. Edge literally became God's "burning bush" to me, and I left class that day with a renewed confirmation that God indeed was calling me to preach in the local church. Up until that day, I had been running from that calling. But now, Jonah had returned to Nineveh. Thankfully, God had used a wonderful professor and not a whale to convince me.

So, with excitement and joy, Pam and I agreed to be considered. There were forty-five people in all that made up our first congregation. I was completely inexperienced in leading a church, but for the next ten-and-one-half years, God would shape us into "Reverend and Mrs. Tim Maynard." Or, as they were fond of calling us, "Brother Tim and Pam."

Upon their invitation to come as pastor, the question of ordination emerged. I petitioned my home church, and the pastor there, Marion Duncan, who had baptized me as a nine-year-old. Revival had come to our home church under his leadership and I had received and listened eagerly to his teaching on cassette tapes. I concluded that, if there was some reason I should not be allowed into ministry, he would have no problem telling me. I was still looking for some reason why I should not be a pastor!

I was ordained in June, 1982. The day of my ordination, I was to attend a council where I would be interviewed for my theological readiness, and then during a formal service that evening I would be charged as a pastor and preach my first sermon as a "reverend." The ordination council took two hours. I've learned since that this length of time was unusual. But back then, they had sent me a one hundred question "study guide" to get ready for the Q and A.

It was a truly holy moment for me and Pam. Our families had gathered (my father, a deacon, served on my ordination

Tim and Pam in front of the sign at Oakland Avenue Baptist Church announcing his ordination service that night.

council), and afterwards I sat, alone, on a front and center pew while the good pastor thundered a sermon just to me concerning the qualifications, behavior and honor of being a minister of the Gospel. I knew in that moment how Joshua must have felt being charged by Moses to lead the people of Israel.

I preached that evening in my home church and following the sermon, I was evaluated by the pastor. He blessed what I had preached and especially complimented me for "using a lot of Scripture" in my sermon. If I needed a sign from God, this was it. And we were off to find our way as Reverend and Mrs Maynard. I was now the shepherd of God's little flock.

And then there were three: Pam and Tim snuggle with Allison.

AND THEN THERE
WERE THREE

L ife was beginning to turn sunnier for us. Some of our "worse" was beginning to turn into "better!" My illness, though still active, was in better check than it had been in over two years. Strength began to return after that dark and difficult season. We had been voted on unanimously by the church and I was to begin as their pastor in May of 1982.

My first official service at the church was a Wednesday night. Earlier that day, we found out that Pam was expecting our first child. It was joyous to announce on my very first night before the church that we were expecting a baby! We had decided if it was a girl, we would name her Amanda Lynn. Then, after we had shared that idea with a couple of friends, we stepped back and listened to the name. (Someone had asked, "Oh...like the Bluegrass instrument?"). We quickly changed it to Allison Leigh. Our little girl was born January 8, 1983.

In a funny turn, I actually got to tell Pam that she was going

Tim was quite comfortable with baby Allison on his chest.

to have a baby. She had taken a pregnancy test and, before there was time to see the results, she had to leave for work. I almost dropped the indicator when it showed a "donut" shape, meaning the test was positive. Our deal was, I would call into the operating room and ask for her if the test was positive. We had been through many negatives and disappointing results. So, if I did not call within the hour (no cell phones then), it was another negative. If I called, she would know it was positive. I called. The operating room erupted in cheers, and Pam left the room in tears. It was a glorious moment.

And now there were three! We were parents, and truly felt like a family. I was now a Daddy! Pam excelled at many things, but few better than being a mother. She was attentive, conscientious, and educated herself about all things relating to child-rearing as she went through her pregnancy. Those were exciting days, filled with anticipation and busyness as we started serving as the pastor's family.

BECOMING FAMILY

Our church sat at the intersection of Highway 61 and Bardstown Road in Lebanon Junction, Kentucky (hence the name, Bardstown Junction). We were within eyesight of one of the largest and most historic Jim Beam distilleries in their system, and twenty miles west of Bardstown, Kentucky. Our building sat squarely in the middle of a soybean field, surrounded by hills and...well, nothing. A few scattered houses paralleled Horsefly Hollow Road, where we were ultimately to live for nine months housesitting for some friends who were on a mission trip. Dividing our church property from Horsefly Hollow was a much-used line of railroad track, and the railroad folks managed to send a train by every Sunday about 11:45 a.m., which signaled its arrival with a loud horn. You could set your clock by it. The people in the pew usually did. It meant I had fifteen minutes to get done. The good news was it woke some of them up.

The church water supply was a rain-fed cistern which collected water in a huge concrete tank, doubling as the back porch of the church building. I did not know what a "cistern" was, and my first shot at defining a cistern was to think it was the female version of "brethren." Not being funny here. I really thought that was what it was. Obviously I was not a country boy.

After Allison's birth as we continued attending Southern Seminary, our lives changed drastically. We became the center of attention and excitement at the apartment complex where we lived, being the only couple with a baby. We had continuous offers for free childcare. Allison was literally born into a loving community at seminary, and she was also the first baby born to anyone at our church in over a decade...the first ever to a pastor and wife in the church's history.

So under Pam's expert mothering hand and Allison Leigh's immersion into an immediate socialization process, it was no wonder to me that she grew up accustomed to being the center of a lot of people's world (with numerous self-proclaimed "adoptive" grandparents), and later married a pastor. In spite of the continual adulation of people, she grew to be a wonderfully well-adjusted little girl with curly blond hair and a winsome personality. She would stand on the pews at the end of the service, holding hands with those around her and singing "I'm so glad I'm a part of the family of God" at the top of her lungs as each service ended. Frankly, we were all glad to be a part. We also were credited with "beginning" the baby boom in the mid-1980s in that part of the world. Before we knew it, young families attending the church became pregnant, and others with preschool children began to attend. We had no place to put them since they'd never had babies there before.

Some of my most cherished memories in that joyful little

congregation are of Pam's early days as our (only) preschool Sunday School teacher. Meeting in the dingy basement of our sanctuary (not far from my dingy-er study), she feverishly read up on the latest preschool techniques, attended conferences offered by our Baptist association and state convention, and soon began leading those conferences.

Her nursing expertise quickly made her an "expert" on every childhood illness in the community. Mostly, she prescribed a syrup that would make the child throw up whatever they had swallowed accidentally. Our children both knew something of the taste of that syrup! She became a "missionary" children's doctor to our Appalachian community.

Though she continued working as a surgical nurse after Allison was born, she had reduced her hours to part-time, a status she maintained for the remainder of her career. As she worked diligently in Sunday School, she would rush to the platform in the sanctuary when the bell rang to get ready for worship...first, as church pianist and later as organist.

In those earliest years of child-rearing, Pam took on the lion's share of the responsibility. She did so, first, because I got out of the way and let her. But Pam seemed to know what she was doing and I didn't have a clue. I became what parenting expert John Rosemond called "a parenting associate."

Second, she was trying to take the burden off of me since I was immersed in school work, writing papers for my master's degree and later for the doctoral program at Southern Seminary. My pastoral workload was increasing, as our church grew to the point that a new sanctuary had to be built.

I say some of this to my regret. Frankly, I did not know

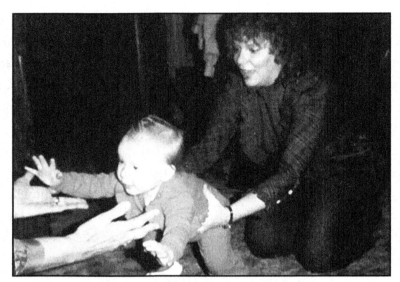

Baby Allison reaches for Daddy as Mommy steadies her balance.

what to say "no" to in those early days, being a consummate people-pleaser by temperament. I was "making a living" now for the family, and I defaulted much of my part of the parenting load to Pam. Though I tried to make up for it when Allison and later when David grew older, I wish I had not missed so many of those early experiences. A clue to young fathers....the mother of your children really didn't sign up to be a one -person show. She wants, values, and needs your help! Just a word to the wise!

Allison was a delight as a little girl (well, not to say she isn't now). She was talkative and precocious, and a born politician. Everyone in the church thought they were her favorite, and it always paid off at Christmas and birthdays! She was comfortable with her celebrity status, and actually thrived on it.

THEN THERE WERE FOUR

T hough we never thought we would get pregnant the first time (we were married five years before Allie came along), we were shocked and pleasantly surprised when, in 1984, we found that we were going to have a second child!

David Hilton was born on February 19, 1985. Just over two years apart, we began immediately to see the differences in our children. Allison's birth was filled with drama, and she was delivered in a rush, after Pam had been in labor all day. The emergency took place when it was found the umbilical cord had wrapped around her neck cutting off her air supply. There was much relief and weeping in the room when she was born and we heard her first cries but she had arrived two weeks early, and spent several days in NICU under the lamps until her liver fully developed.

Dave was a breach baby. Just a few weeks before her due date, Pam was involved in a collision on an icy bridge while traveling to work. The jarring of the wreck, they told us, probably forced our baby into a breach position. The obstetrician set a date

The four of us: Tim, Pam, Allison and newborn David.

for a C-section, and while I stood in the room holding Pam's hand (not normal procedure but she knew people), our son David Hilton was placed crying into my arms as they closed the incision. I got to hold him before she did!

Now we were four. A boy and a girl were now ours and due to some medical complications we decided not to attempt to have more. But for us, we already had the perfect family. David Hilton (named for me and his "Uncle" Hilton Davis, one of our best friends who along with his wife Jane helped raise our kids), was an absolutely perfect "fit" for us. Allison quickly began to assume the role of big sister, boss, and interpreter for what "David" wanted when he couldn't clearly ask for it himself. She had the gift of "interpreting tongues" as he learned to talk.

GREEN ACRES IS THE PLACE TO BE

Our family survived four moves before we owned our first house. Our newly purchased 1300 square foot "mansion" was located on five acres of property which we found later was worth far more than the house. It was built with enough space between the cedar-shingle siding and foundation to allow all of our heat to escape in the winter and for mice to come and go freely...which they did.

The house, bought at auction, was heated by wood and kerosene stoves. I became expert at collecting, stacking, and chopping wood. I also learned what a septic tank was, (and why flowers grew so well in a "certain" section of the yard), and also why people really don't want to have an iron well to supply water to their home. The house was built by a couple who had violently divorced, and marks of that violence and neglect were evident. I had my work cut out for me inside the house, and also had an acre and a half of lawn to cut and tend.

While Beech Grove Road was a quiet country road with just a few houses sprinkled around, it was anything but quiet all the time. Just to our southeast over a range of hills that surrounded our community was the Fort Knox military installation. Since it housed armored divisions, it also had areas for large ordinance target practice. The biggest guns we had in our arsenal in the US Army were tested just over twenty miles beyond our home. That meant some nights were lit up like an unending thunderstorm as we watched the flashes and heard the muffled explosions and low roar of tank-mounted machine guns. Pictures were always askew on the walls, since the seemingly non-stop firing shook the very foundation of our home.

I often would take my lunch time to come home, hop on my junked-out lawn tractor, and circle the acreage in my dress pants, shirt and tie. Pam would come to the door and sing the "Green Acres" theme song to tease me. In an early version of multi-tasking, I got a small wagon and hooked it to the back of the lawn tractor and hauled the kids around for free rides as I cut the grass.

David was always holding on to his latest acquisition: a dinosaur or one of his many "guys," as he called them. Sometimes a GI Joe soldier, or sometimes a monster or superhero would be his favorite. He had gotten a Teddy Ruxpin talking teddy bear one Christmas and that was a favorite until he baptized it in the tub. Teddy Ruxpin never spoke to us again. David loved Christmas, and we learned later that "gifts" is one of his dominant love languages. He loved getting money, but only because he knew he could buy himself the latest superhero or accessory to play with. A saver he was not.

Our children were amazingly well-behaved, even in church

when Pam and I were preoccupied up front leading worship. Pam planned activities for them...coloring, drawing, games or flannel "quiet books"...and services would fly by for them even though they weren't sitting with us. Childcare during church didn't exist then for us...you were on your own! So they took turns sitting with different adults and never caused us a moment's distraction. Well, hardly ever.

Both of our children made early professions of faith and were baptized at Bardstown Junction. I was privileged to baptize them both. I am glad for that, and I know that for both, their decisions were sincere. Their earliest discipleship was done in the midst of a loving church community.

Even during our "vacations" (which is what we called traveling home for four hours to visit our parents during school breaks), they learned to be content playing, and sometimes Pam planned car games for them to keep them preoccupied. (When that didn't work, she dosed them with allergy medication that helped them sleep...a consummate nurse). In spite of the ongoing demands on her mind with her profession, "churching" and volunteer work, and being a musician and pastor's wife she never lost her focus and priority on Allison and Dave. They always got the best from her, and that would be a trait that did not cease as they got older.

Pam's philosophy of family life was that it was to be a seamless unit. It was us four, if necessary, standing against the world. Many times that philosophy was a necessary one. Our parents lived four hours away, so we couldn't always count on their help.

Though our kids would have times when they began to go

The Maynard family in one of their church portraits.

their own way as adolescents, we still would find time to be together as family.

One of my favorite memories with our children growing up was something we came up with to engage us all. We would play Charades using characters in the Bible. This ensured their full physical, mental and spiritual engagement as we acted out Old and New Testament characters and their stories.

We had precious times at bedtime as we "said" our prayers and told Bible stories or sometimes sang a simple chorus or hymn. Often Pam would serenade our children to sleep with soft piano strains from her repertoire of music.

We enjoyed, even in their last years of high school and early college years (since both were still home), playing games with our family. One in particular, which Pam created, was a card game in which we used quarters as tokens. This game, called "31," occupied a lot of hours together in the kitchen after supper was done. We decided the first person out got to clean up the dishes! But even after the "loser" had finished, nobody wanted to leave the table, and other times the game would be followed up with conversations about life and what it meant to live out our faith... (and a few hard lessons about gambling).

I need to say in print here that our children have always...ALWAYS...been amazingly flexible and adaptable, even in the worst of times. They have consistently given us grace and understanding even in times of sacrifice. Without a manual to go by, they have lived a faithful life as "PK's — aka Pastors Kids" — and did not grow up resenting either the Lord's church, rejecting the faith, or turning their backs on us. I will never outlive my gratitude for my children and the lives they have faithfully lived

Dave, Tim and Allison

since leaving their father's house. Only God could have loved them more than we did. And no father or mother could be prouder of them and the lives they are living now with their own families.

While it's easy to forget the times when things did not go well in our family, I would have to honestly say with perspective that those times were very rare. No family is perfect, and I am happy that ours was a refuge not only for our children, but for me as well.

We have a godly wife and loving mother to thank for that.

PART 4

FLORIDA OR BUST

The Maynards as they looked coming to Florida in 1992.

TRANSITIONS

In 1990, I (finally) concluded my career as a student. It had spanned two years at Cumberland College, followed by ten years at Southern Seminary since that day we ate pizza on the front porch of our trailer for the last time. It was now our thirteenth year together as husband and wife... becoming one.

I was tired of being a student, and Pam was tired of being married to one. So with graduation of 1990, I walked across the stage at Southern's historic Mullins Chapel and received the piece of paper that proclaimed I could now legitimately be called "Doctor."

Pam had a desk plaque especially made at Louisville Stoneware (her favorite store in Louisville), made of blue and white ceramic glass with "Dr Tim Maynard" hand-painted on it. I was very proud of it. My family teasingly called me "Dr Tim" and "Dr Dad" and "Dr Darling" for about a week, and then they were over it.

I began getting "itchy" feet and felt discontent almost

immediately, and in fact I had begun to do so during the defense of my doctoral project. It was time to move out of our backroads, idyllic country church— as contented and happy as we had been there—and find a church ready to embrace the future and go places. So the search began.

The doors I thought would quickly open when I produced a doctoral degree closed in my face almost as quickly. In fact, no less than three churches voted me down (virtually unheard of in Baptist life) for a variety of reasons. But in the process of talking to the last two, I was contacted, out of the blue it seemed, by a church in Jacksonville, Florida. If Alex Trebek had asked me the question on Jeopardy, I could not have told him where Jacksonville, Florida even was located. I just knew it wasn't in Kentucky and so, despite some protracted but rich conversations with the pulpit committee chairman, I politely declined. I had already told God my plan: To go anywhere He wanted me to go as long as I didn't have to leave Kentucky. Surely Florida could not be His will for us. Wasn't that like a foreign country? Did I have to learn another language? I hadn't signed on to be a missionary.

The churches that had reached out to me, sometimes from the recommendation of trusted friends or inside contacts, shut their respective doors. Churches that I thought would be glad, indeed...HONORED to have a newly-minted doctoral graduate were suspicious of the orthodoxy of the institution from which I had just graduated. But by then we were so ready to move that when a church contacted us from Alaska, we went to the library and checked out books to show the kids what Alaska looked like.

After the third turndown, the pulpit committee from

Florida called again. This was the third time from 1991 to 1992 they had contacted me. On this occasion, they simply asked "Can we come and listen to you preach?" A pew of five or six more people on a Sunday to beef up morning attendance wasn't a bad thing in a small church. Attendance would spike almost ten percent. So I said, "Certainly."

They came on a Sunday that I was preaching on finances which, apparently, went well. We "snuck" to lunch after church with the gathering of strangers and they told me of their genuine conviction that they believed I was to come as their next pastor. While I didn't share their enthusiasm, I was out of options. My contacts had dried up. My doctorate was withering on the vine. I was now almost thirty-eight and life was speeding past while I went nowhere tending sheep on the backroads. So I looked at Pam, and then to the chairman and said, "We'll come and visit."

The next week we received two plane tickets in the mail. The intriguing thing for me and for Pam was that we had never flown in an airplane before. Never needed to. Never really thought much about it. Now, we were booked on a November flight to Florida.

We left wearing sweaters and winter wear when we departed from Louisville's chilly international airport. In a few hours, we landed in Florida heat and humidity that had us almost disrobing before we got to the terminal.

The committee chairman eagerly met us and took us directly to a hotel room in Mandarin (wait...isn't that in China??) where we would stay the next few days. A basket of goodies awaited us in the room. I was impressed. Pam still looked stunned. I wrote it off to jet lag.

Later that day, a van met us packed with new "friends" who populated the search team. It was their job to convince us that we were the right family for the job. I got my first look at Mandarin and then, taking our breath away, we crossed the Julington Creek bridge. They told us, "This is just a creek. Wait until you see the river!" It looked, and now started to feel, like paradise on earth.

We came off the bridge and drove onto a tight two-lane road with, well, nothing much on it. No traffic. A grocery store called "Food Lion" was on the left hand side and across the street the local watering hole, identified on a crude black and white sign as "Smitty's Bar." Ahead on the left was a large wooden sign with green letters that welcomed all to "Fruit Cove Baptist Church."

I was disappointed the first time I saw the campus. We had visualized a much larger, more urban campus and newer structure and this looked like our little church in Kentucky, except this was surrounded by palmetto shrubs and scruffy pine trees rather than soybean plants. At least there was no train nearby.

I tried to smile and make pleasant conversation but inside was deeply disappointed. So was Pam, she told me later. No wonder they hadn't sent us pictures. After a quick tour of the two buildings, and a further disappointing visit into the sanctuary, which looked run down and filled with disheveled, white-cushioned chairs scattered everywhere, I had pretty much decided I was right the first time to turn them down. Now, it's going to be much harder to do. I secretly wondered if we were supposed to pay them back for the plane tickets if we said no?

We went next to the "mission field," and there we saw

homes...some older and, behind the church, a development called "Julington Creek Plantation" that had begun but was halted when the owner of the company had ended up on 60 Minutes...and in jail...just a few months prior to our visit.

But what we could not deny was an electricity in the van when the committee spoke of their vision and what the community was going to become when the construction begins again. I had heard it all before. That's why I came to Bardstown Junction over a decade before, and the lack of growth was why I now wanted to leave.

I think they could see our disappointment when they dropped us off again at the hotel. We had a few hours before the evening meal, where we would meet the rest of the committee members and their families. I sat brooding in the hotel room, trying to come up with ways to tell them why they really don't want us here. Pam just wanted to go home.

What we didn't realize at that moment was...we already were.

THE FATEFUL MEAL

I call it "the meal" because of its importance to us. Pam and I thereafter referred to it as "the meal." It took place in the home of an older couple on the committee. She was a graduate of Southern Seminary's music school herself. At least I had one friendly voice to defend my alma mater.

The meal took place south of Orangedale in a lovely home on the St John's River within view of the Shand's Bridge. It featured fresh shrimp caught from their boat dock behind the house (impressive!) and accompanied by smoked brisket. I remember it so well. We gathered around the table, and really enjoyed the company of the family members there. It felt like a homecoming or family reunion instead of a meal at which I was about to be the main course.

Coffee and dessert and conversation soon followed in the living room. The committee began once again pouring out their hearts about what they believed the Lord was going to do through their church. It was staggering to hear them, frankly. One of the members then told us the story of how they had at least two pastors they had interviewed in this season who had been voted on by the church on Sunday night, and invited to come. The pastor would accept, and then on Monday morning call and turn them down. The committee and church, of course, would be crushed. And just for the record, that was as unheard of as a church voting no on a prospective candidate. We had all obviously been "dating" the wrong people.

But members of the committee told us that, from the first time they got our information and some sample sermon tapes, they knew I was going to be their next pastor. So they took each turndown by a pastor as another confirmation that I was supposed to be the one to come. So they would call again, not knowing that I had just been rejected each time before they called.

The excuses I had carefully crafted earlier in the day began to feel like sand in my mouth. I couldn't speak them aloud. I spent a lot of time looking at the floor as they spoke, humbled by what they were saying, frightened but at the same time burning inside with the growing awareness that this was to be our church. I prayed in that meeting, "God if you're about to move us to Florida, you get to tell Pam."

It was then that I looked up and looked over into the face of my bride...a face to my surprise that was now streaming with tears. God had spoken to her, too, as often happens with soulmates. And within that brief moment, our lives changed ... yet again.

FLORIDA, HERE WE COME!

We were asked to return to Florida the first week of December 1992. We spent a long weekend, flying in with our kids from Louisville on Thursday. We missed church that Sunday, and I had decided it was most honest to tell them where we were going ... and why.

We looked at a few houses, visited the campus of Julington Creek Elementary School where Allison and Dave would attend (since it was the only elementary school around), and began a busy round of weekend dinners and meetings. Each confirmed to us more deeply that this was God's will for us.

The meetings were almost a rubber stamp of the committee's recommendation, but to due diligence each had to take place. We met Sunday School classes, deacons, and the two staff members (one part-time). I met with the deacons and was asked to cast my vision for the church. I don't believe I had one yet, so I just echoed what the committee had said. It worked.

Sunday morning I preached (I frankly don't remember what), and returned on Sunday night to meet with the one hundred and six adults who would cast their vote. The committee stood and made the formal recommendation to the body that I be considered as their next pastor. The church prayed and our family was dismissed and sequestered in the pastor's study in an adjacent building.

We awaited our fate. The church met a few moments before they asked us to return to the sanctuary for the outcome of the vote. The total: one hundred for and six against.

It was not unanimous, but it was better than anything I had gotten in the last few go-rounds in other churches! We said "yes" to the affirmation and applause of the one hundred. (I was trying to look around to see who wasn't clapping to find the "six" who voted against me...just couldn't find them).

The next morning, the committee chairman called my room and asked, "You haven't changed your mind have you?" I laughed and said, "not yet." Pam and I were together on our decision and our children were excited for the move that would relocate us over seven hundred and fifty miles from our home. It wasn't missions but a move to Africa...or Alaska...wouldn't have felt much different to us. We had stood at the airport before in Louisville and watched as a missionary family we had befriended in seminary left with their three children, waving goodbye to their families for three years. I was starting to feel that same twinge of sadness that I saw in their eyes and the eyes of their family.

Pam and the children were to fly out later Monday, while I would stay behind to begin a search for a place to live. I had to buy a house...alone...soon. There are so many ways this could

David and Allison were PK (pastor's kids) but they
were seldom out of line. Their parents were thankful.

have gone sideways, but Pam gave me very specific guidelines concerning what she wanted. I found the house, the third I looked at, that met those qualifications. Since I had no requirements it worked for me.

I signed an offer for a starter home in the Remington Forest subdivision on Tuesday afternoon, walked through the house taping with my video camera (the size of a small suitcase) and then rented a car to drive back to Kentucky. We were going to be property owners in Florida. But for now, we had to determine how to tell our church back home...and our families...the news.

SKIPPING CHRISTMAS

We returned to our church family in Kentucky the second Sunday of December, 1992 with heavy hearts. Being the pastor's family is very much like a marriage...sometimes a good one and sometimes not. Ours, thankfully, had been a healthy one. But now, we were about to bring the news that we were "breaking up" and that God had called us to a new church family to love and serve.

I didn't really understand how hard this hit our little congregation until I returned some twenty-five years later, following Pam's death. They had asked me in the spring of 2017 if I would come for their One Hundredth Anniversary, and I initially said no...not knowing the outcome of Pam's condition. This was the first time they had "formally" invited us to return. And when I arrived I found out why.

They were hurt by our leaving. They never understood why we left. Some had been hurt and angry for years (twenty-four if we're counting). The homecoming was a time of healing for them and with them. Allison had returned to "her" church of origin for the service. There were hundreds of hugs and buckets of tears shed. But I think we also left with healing in the wake of this visit. It was needed. And as they sought to comfort me in the midst of that service, they found the healing they needed as well. I was saddened that it took Pam's death for that to happen.

Our notice to move was by necessity short. The committee in Florida was anxious for us to sign final documents on the house and spend our first night there by the end of the year to qualify for the Homeowner's Tax Exemption status. That meant we would be packing and preparing to load a moving truck...over Christmas. The first, and only Christmas our family ever missed. It brought to life for us the reality of the very first Christmas, as Jesus "moved' to earth to take on the flesh and blood of humanity. Additionally, when Jesus arrived He was placed in the arms of a dislocated family who was forced to travel for a tax census. Mary did so as she was experiencing her ninth month of pregnancy. We reminded ourselves as we recounted the Christmas Story for our children that we had very little to complain about.

I still remember the sad little tree that Pam had propped up for the kids on the top of one of our moving boxes. If I remember correctly, they didn't seem to care. They just wanted to know if Santa would still visit us in the mess.

He did. Christmas of 1992 was a white one that year...one of the few we had seen. Our excitement overwhelmed the normal emotion of the season. When I arrived home after "house hunting" in Florida with the video tape, we slipped it in the player and watched our new home through the screen of a small TV set in our living room early on a chilly December morning. It quickly became our family's favorite and most requested "show" to watch as we imagined how our sparse furniture would look and as the kids began to mentally "decorate" their rooms.

The day after Christmas we finished packing boxes and began a long train of goodbyes from our church in Kentucky. We had already tearfully said our goodbyes to our families at home the day before. Now our spiritual family that had nurtured us through student years and early parenting met us at the door with small gifts to take with us: Christmas candies and bread and other goodie bags for the kids to open on our upcoming twelve -hour - plus drive.

We asked Allison and Dave what they wanted to do in Kentucky before we left. They decided they wanted to sleigh ride down the sloping hill across the street from our house. So we borrowed the needed equipment, suited them up in winter gear, and turned them loose; hoping they would exhaust themselves before the long ride.

The only person exhausted was me...and we solemnly shut the door on our Dodge Caravan, and pointed it south on Interstate 65. Our ride soon grew quiet, and I know Pam and I were reflecting on good memories of our time there. We were ready for our new adventure to begin, but not without shedding a lot of grateful tears for those who helped prepare us for this next leg of our journey.

A NEW BEGINNING

Our first night in Florida was less than glamorous. The moving company had decided to move our belongings in two trucks. It was not because we had so much, but because they already had another home packed on the truck and going to Florida as well. They stuffed our few boxes and little bit of furniture in the cracks and crevices of the truck. And they quickly ran out of space.

The first load made it to Florida on December 30... thankfully the one with mattresses on it. So we slept on our mattresses on the floor the last two days of 1992. The kids were having a blast with it, so we tried to enjoy it and get along.

On December 30th we visited the local bank used by our church. Wachovia was, actually, the "only show in town" at that time. It made the choice pretty easy. And when we walked in (they introduced us as "Dr. and Mrs. Maynard") the tellers grew quiet. They stared at us as though they didn't know what to say. A lady scurried and offered us a drink.

Apparently our finance committee brought some pretty heavy pressure to bear on the bank's manager and later we learned it's president. They told me that in their history at Wachovia, they had never seen a closing come together so quickly. And in hindsight, it was pretty amazing that they pulled it off.

Had they only known how much I was freaking out on the inside. We were signing documents on a home valued at over $100,000...a sum that was more than twice the value of the house we were selling in Kentucky. God better know what He was doing because I was about to go into major league, mind-shattering debt.

But I tried to look cool and collected as I signed my life away, and as Pam joined me. As yet, she had not begun working with Mayo Clinic and we had decided for the first couple of months to let her stay home and get the house together and to get the kids acclimated to this new world.

Speaking of which, I preached the first Sunday of January, 1993. It was indeed a strange new world as we were reminded by the humidity in January and as I watched palm trees waving outside the windows of the sanctuary. Where in the world was I? It felt like I was in a dream.

I began a teaching series on Abraham that Sunday and drew the obvious connections of our journey of letting go of the familiar world of Kentucky and, in obedient and trusting faith, following God to Florida. Deep inside I had the assurance, however, that if I blew it, then Florida was far enough from Kentucky that I could bail out and no one back home would ever know.

Things went well enough our first weeks and months in the Sunshine State. The kids were adjusting well to their new home,

The organ shoes that Pam wore while making beautiful music.

school, and surroundings, and Dave was quickly becoming enamored with alligators.

I got my indication of Pam's discontent after the first couple of months, and learned that she was unhappy not being a part of the music ministry as instrumentalist. Though she sang faithfully in the choir with her lovely alto voice, her heart was aching to play. I realized that, in our marriage, this was the first time she was not on the platform beside me. I needed her there. She missed being engaged in ministry with me.

RE-ORGAN-IZING

Our organist had been hired from another church locally. Her heart did not seem to be into growing in her role at Fruit Cove. She was a pianist who played organ because she was paid to do so. After she had refused yet again to attend choir rehearsals under a new director, she left the music ministry.

Though Pam did not begin immediately, she ultimately auditioned and began playing every Sunday at the request of our pianist, Carolyn Nichols. The hardest thing for her to accept during her ordeal with cancer was no longer being able to play in worship on Sunday. It cut deeply into our identity as a couple and into one of the great gifts she felt she could offer the Lord.

Holding the two pairs of well-worn organ shoes she had used for the past twenty-five years in my hands has been one of the most painful things I've done since Pam's death. Both of us bled from the wound of her being sidelined in her ministry, but obviously it hurt her far worse.

In those earlier days, as the church began to grow beyond

two hundred in worship, we did pretty much everything from leading on Sunday to cleaning up and closing up on Sunday nights. One Christmas Eve service, the first with new dark maroon pews the church had just added, we learned why it's not a good idea to use real candles indoors. We were getting ready to go home and start getting the kids ready for bed, but looking back across the sanctuary after the lights came on, we saw with panic the long white waxy stripes that had dripped down the dark fabric of the pews. So, since everyone else had already left for home, we stayed behind and scrubbed wax out of the pew backs.

But each thing we did was done with growing joy and gratitude for where we were as we followed and trusted the Lord. God had led us home. We didn't know it at the time, but our roots would grow deep in the sandy soil of St. Johns County. In reality our first two years were not ideal. We had several leadership conflicts, and a struggle for control of the direction of the church's mission money of all things.

I had never confronted any conflict that I couldn't fix with a cup of coffee and some straight talk with a farmer or factory worker. But this conflict was bigger than anything I had ever encountered. It threatened to split the church wide open. At the end, several families had left, including two that were our staunchest supporters when we first came. It was the most heartbreaking time I had ever gone through as a pastor. Several times during those long months of infighting, I had investigated what it would take to just fly us out of there and go back to Kentucky.

EXPANDING

But we persevered, and before long celebrated our fourth year with the church. By then, we had gone through a building campaign, since the small sanctuary we worshiped in was filling up two and three times a week. God was moving, and it was exciting!

We built the new sanctuary way too small, seating only 850, but it stretched everything we had in the bank or could raise or borrow to build it. The sanctuary was to be opened for our first service on Easter Sunday morning. The evening before, we were still tweaking the building and cleaning and filling bathroom stalls with toilet paper. It was exciting and I remembered how proud Pam and I were of what God had done through the church in just five short years of our coming.

Our phone rang early that Easter morning in 1997. I was already up and making coffee when we received the call. Our missionary friends, Nik and Ruth Ripken, were calling with the devastating news that their sixteen-year-old middle son Timothy had died the night before in Nairobi from an asthma attack. I could not imagine being hit harder by any news in that moment. The event of their son's death is dramatically portrayed in the book and movie, *The Insanity of God*. We had become good friends with the Ripkens and their boys in school. We would keep their kids, and they kept ours. Nik and I encouraged and nursed and pushed each other through our doctoral work. I stumbled through as best I could in talking to these grieving friends, thousands of miles away from us. If I could, I would have boarded a plane in Jacksonville and flown to Africa to embrace them and stand with them. Nik and I had even "prearranged" a marriage between Timothy and Allison (with their mothers' approval, of course).

The morning of the opening celebration was filled with events and markers of our progress as a church. My parents and Dad's sister flew down from Kentucky to be with us. I was praying alternately for the Ripkens and their boys and family and then praying that God would bring enough people to fill the sanctuary at least once so we wouldn't fall on our face.

And as God often does, He proved that I don't ask big enough. Two services were necessary to house the people who came. Of course, it was Easter. And that day, I had the sorrow and joy of proclaiming both the crucifixion and the resurrection of our Lord and of just how real we wanted that message of resurrection to be to the Ripken's family in Kenya. Our church by now had also met and fallen in love with this wonderful missionary family. We found once again that we must "rejoice with those who rejoice, and weep with those who weep." Both happened that Easter morning.

I look back now in my mind's eye to the front section of the sanctuary where my late father sat with his beloved sister and my mother. My dad and Aunt Margaret would be with the Lord before the next five years unfolded. And I will never forget the sorrow and tears of the announcement about Timothy's passing, mingled with the joy and power of that Easter morning.

And I remember and give thanks again for the power of that message.

IN SICKNESS
AND IN HEALTH

T he years of ministry that took place between the opening of our sanctuary and seems somewhat like a whirlwind...or at least a blur. I told someone once that I felt like the engineer of a train that had already left the station and I was running as hard as I could to get on it!

Along the way, I was invited to join the teaching staff of the New Orleans Seminary Extension Center opening in Jacksonville. They needed a professor of pastoral care and psychology. And so I received a call from their newly appointed director in Jacksonville, Rev. Charles Ragland.

I had briefly met and chatted with Charles since coming to Florida, but this offer both floored and excited me. It fell right in my wheelhouse of degree work, and the idea of working in theological education had often been in the back of my mind. So I said yes.

During the summer before the first semester, I plowed

eagerly through the textbook for the course, and prepared my notes and outlines. That fall term we began with eighteen students in my class. I taught as an adjunct seminary professor for the next ten years. It was a joyful and enriching time for me. In recent months, I have reconnected with students who told me "I still use the stuff you taught us in class." It hit me again, with those statements, how much I loved teaching pastors.

The church loved us well through those early days. Pastor Appreciation Days would find us loaded up with gifts and flowers and cards and gift certificates for wonderful trips. Our favorite was a trip to the Greyfield Inn on Cumberland Island. We loved the secluded beaches, the picnic lunches, and the bike trails that went on forever.

Once we were able to sit on the front porch of the big house where the Kennedy family would vacation. We got to sit and sip lemonade while watching a wild horse give birth in a field just in front of us. I am so glad for those memories, and grateful that Pam and I shared them together.

On our twenty-fifth wedding anniversary, the church surprised us with a trip to Hawaii. We were awe-struck by the generosity and thoughtfulness of our wonderful congregation. Our previous church had to vote each November to give us a $100 gift for Christmas.

During our campaign to build our multipurpose building, a $6 million project, life got really complicated. My father was diagnosed with a strange and aggressive brain tumor we had never heard of called a glioblastoma. This was in the summer months of 2001, just before 9/11. Numerous trips back home were needed to walk with my parents through this terrible

The Maynards at the wedding for Allison and Patrick.

The Maynards at the wedding for Dave and Logan.

experience.

While that was happening, almost simultaneously, I was diagnosed at 47 years of age with prostate cancer. After two separate biopsies during that summer, they determined it was cancer. A diagnosis like that of someone at my age was almost unheard of at the time. So in the last days of my dad's struggle with brain cancer, I began my own battle with prostate cancer and underwent surgery the following October.

This was the first serious diagnosis I had ever experienced. Though ulcerative colitis would still come and go, this was a completely different situation. Pam told me later (when things were better) that she felt in her heart I was going to die. It was a crisis like we had not known since college and her surgery for an ovarian cyst. But again, God was faithful and my illness was "not unto death."

While all of this was happening with church, school, and health circumstances, our kids were growing up. Adolescence had come to live in our home. Remarkably and thankfully we had really good kids who had their bumps here and there but did not let their adolescent years push them away from God or us. They knew our family was in crisis during those days, and seemed to sense that they needed to grow up fast and be there to support and help. And they did.

Allison and Dave both were dating some, but Allison was the first to get 'serious' with a boy. After a couple of less than ideal relationships, she met Patrick whose family was from Middleburg, Florida across the river. She and Patrick started dating and, I believe, fell for each other pretty quickly. Patrick stated from the beginning of their relationship that he wanted to be a pastor. Allison stated from the beginning she wanted to be married to a pastor. (I secretly felt smug, because the fact that she wanted to be a pastor's wife meant that I hadn't messed up too bad).

Dave began dating and, like Allison, had a couple of relationships that weren't lasting. But then he met "the girl next door;" a lovely girl that he had been with in church for some time. They started dating and fell for each other pretty quickly as well. Logan Cubilla and her family had been attending Fruit Cove almost from the beginning of our tenure in the church. It's interesting that, like me, Dave had looked all over the country for his girlfriends and ended up falling in love with "the girl next door."

Our kids were happy God had led us to Florida so they could meet their destined mates. It was bittersweet watching our children grow up into young adults who were needing us less and less. And then we remembered that this was exactly what we had been praying for as our family grew. Who would have thought that on our first day in the Sunshine State over twenty years before, we would be planning their weddings here.

AND THEN
THERE WERE SEVEN?

No, we didn't have a another child. We had a granddaughter! McCail Violet came blitzing into our lives in June of 2016. Dave and Logan's firstborn landed in our lives and changed...well, everything for us. Our family had grown from four, then to six, and now to seven.

I became Poppy, and Pam became Mamaw...so chosen after the name of her favorite grandmother. My name just meant... Poppy. She became the light and focus of our months before Pam's diagnosis. It was always her intention to retire from nursing to move into caring for McCail as our children worked.

Watching Dave and Logan handle and raise their daughter so wonderfully has been one of the greatest sources of pride and joy we have ever felt, and being called a grandfather and grandmother has been the crowning moment of our adult lives. I wrote the following within hours of McCail Violet's birth:

It happened just like I was told it would. They warned me....well-meaning veterans of this world I stepped into today....but I really didn't believe all the hype. I mean, come on. How could this event change my life the way they said it would...changing everything around me? I am, after all, a rational, professional, fairly educated human being. I just won't get swept away the way that many predicted I would.....at least not to the extent I had been told it would.

I pondered this as I sat with other expectant family members in the Family Retreat at Baptist South on Sunday and Monday. Waiting. Eating junk food. Playing card games and watching endless re-runs of game shows. Jumping every time the door to the Labor and Delivery floor came open. Reaching for another of those devilish Hot Tamale candies I am now addicted to. (Thank you Ashley!!)

Frankly, I knew it would be moving. But life-changing? For me? Wasn't sure how that really could happen. And then, at the end of over 24 hours of labor and waiting, my son Dave sent us a snapshot from his phone inside the room. The baby was here! Three days after her due date, she almost stuck the landing. And she was born on my Dads birthday!

After our first excited rounds of texts and phone calls were made, and great-grandparents and aunts and uncles were notified of their new "promotion," something incredible happened. My son walked into the waiting room and for the very first time I saw it. He was a father.

Tim and Pam with McCail.

It showed on his face, weary after a sleepless night and standing alongside his wife. I was filled with a pride for him at that moment that was beyond description. He was now different. I could see it. We embraced for a moment and he disappeared behind the double doors with two weary and anxious grandmothers and a newly minted aunt.

The other grandfather and I sat in the room waiting for our invitation to go back and meet our new granddaughter. We were both aware that grandpa's take a back seat in moments like this, and we were ok with that. Paul and I chatted as we waited thumbing mindlessly through an AARP magazine. I looked for another Hot Tamale. Sadly, there were none.

Then it was our turn to enter. I walked into a room

to the sound of the baby crying as Dave changed her diaper. Knowing it would be the first of many thousands, I knew he would become adept at this skill.

I surveyed the emotion-packed room as a spirit that I can only describe as God-sent joy was pervasive. I saw it in the new mother's face. Logan is a beautiful woman, but as she lay in the bed disheveled by the hours of labor she had undergone, I saw a radiance and beauty in her that was remarkable. She was a mother. She was now different. I could see it. I could feel it around her.

Then I had the privilege of watching as my son carefully handed his now-swaddled, contented, perfectly- formed, lovely, dark-haired daughter to my wife. And as I watched, Pam changed as she carefully and adoringly held her newly born granddaughter in her arms. A joy and beauty emanated from her that made me love her in a way that I had not experienced before. She literally radiated with joy. She was a grandmother! She was now different. I could see it in her eyes, her face. I could sense it in her spirit.

By now my eyes were so tear-filled that the room was blurred. I had to step aside to clear them. Because then they said, "Poppy, it's your turn to hold her." And when they handed her to me, I changed. I could feel it from the depths of my being....a love and joy flowing out that only a caring Creator-God and a beautiful newborn baby could bring. As I looked into the beauty of McCail Violet's face, I was now different.

I am a grandfather. And I am certain my life will never be quite the same! Poppy

None could have been crazier about a child's birth than my wife. She so loved this baby, months and months before she was born. We would receive weekly updates on our iPhones from Logan on the progress and "size" of the baby as she grew. Logan was a beautiful mother, going through the pregnancy with little complaint or complication. Dave was a doting and caring father before McCail ever appeared.

But no grandmother was ever more thrilled to welcome a baby than was Pam. Months before she spent every free moment sewing little bibs and other "baby things" so "her" grandchild would have personalized, handmade things. We shopped for and bought enough clothing for McCail's first three years.

God's timing is always perfect...synced up with His Divine purposes, events unfold on the stage of world history. But the concern of His timing is not only for large, earth-shaking events. No, it also concerns the details of the birth of a child...the timing of a life coming to earth in just the right moment.

McCail Violet, I believe, was the product of just such Divine planning and wisdom. Her presence, her joy, her spirit spilled out in our lives in such force and abundance that I can only say she was sent from God for just such a time as this. Though frail and small, her life became a lifeline and a conduit of hope to both Pam and me through these difficult days. God knew.

Dave was entering summer break as a high school art teacher at Nease High School in St. Johns, Florida. He would be the primary caregiver for his almost one-year-old child in the coming months since Logan was back returning to work full-time.

He asked me, "Dad, what do you want me to do for Mom and you in this time?" I told him, "Dave, the most important thing you can do right now is raise our granddaughter and let us visit with her when you can. That is your priority." He was generous with his time and visits with McCail and each visit renewed Pam's...and my hope. I don't know what we would have done without her and our son's loving care for his mother...and our granddaughter in this journey.

PART 5

THE CRUSHING

Tim's devotion to Pam was heartfelt from the beginning.

KNOCKED DOWN BUT NOT KNOCKED OUT

The preceding pages encapsulated forty years of life together. Forty years of loving, of working, of deciding, of living, of serving God and others, of learning, of growing, and of child rearing. Each of these experiences provided a brick in the foundation of our life together...our "two-becoming-one" experience.

But what follows is more slow motion than fly-over. It contains memories, blogs, and reflections of the illness and subsequent death of my wife. Some walked with us through much of this, but for others this may be the first time you have heard the story. I have written this tearfully, joyfully, gratefully. I am learning after some months to experience gratitude for the incredible woman I shared my life with, and not just to experience the pain of separation from her.

C.S. Lewis said, "to love anything is to be vulnerable." When you love, your heart is open...not only to the many notes

Pam made this birthday card for Tim on June 11, the last one she would celebrate with her husband.

of the song that God sings in pleasure over you, but also to the minor keys...and the rests that come in silence. Love involves sacrifice...and risk. You can, and likely will, get hurt in the process of loving.

And yet the joy that comes from genuinely loving another human soul is a far greater reward...even when pain meets us or death visits. "We love, because He first loved us."

MORTALITY CHECK

E ven as a couple stands at a wedding altar in the early blush of romance, beginning life's journey hand in hand, most know that the spectre of death can visit without warning. I have presided over many funerals where the spouse who lay in the casket was far too young to be taken from his or her mate. With our work in ministry and Pam's career in nursing care, facing death was a constant focus of what we did. I had even, with gallows humor, suggested that we buy and operate a "marrying and burying parlor" to operate in retirement (and yes, those do exist).

But the truth still lingers that death can rip apart a couple's existence, and there is no chance to appeal its decision. The "last enemy to be destroyed" still has its days of seeming victory. "But thanks be to God who gives us the victory through our Lord Jesus Christ."

We had several times faced the possibility that death could come to us. I had already been through cancer surgery. That time of our lives ripped both of us open to the possibility that, one day, death would likely take one of us. But until the word "cancer" is spoken with your name attached, that time seems like a distant future.

During my years of pastoral training, I had a phrase that attached itself to me and I've used it and thought about it often. The phrase is "mortality check." It is that "gut check" moment when we look into a casket at the face of someone we knew and maybe loved...and now they're dead. Is this even possible? Could this happen...to ME? That's a mortality check...a reminder that we are frail, that...as the Bible puts it...we are "like a mist that appears one day and is gone the next."

Pam also was diagnosed with thyroid cancer several years ago, at Christmas time. We attended a Christmas party at the Mayo Clinic for the surgical team of which she was a part. The doctor who would perform her surgery was there with us. Her determination was to perform in the Christmas musical the next night at church, and then on Monday morning to go for her surgery. She had to undergo follow-up radiation, and every annual scan brought the icy fingers of the possibility of cancer's recurrence back to our consciousness.

With these experiences as part of our history, we stopped taking life for granted. However, none of that prepared us in the least for what was about to happen. In 2017, in the year of our fortieth wedding anniversary, our life ground to a halt. Death threatened once again to tear our lives apart. This time the prospect of its winning was much worse.

In November of 2016, following a nasty bout with the flu, Pam began to experience numbness in the tip of the index finger of her left hand. This persisted through the holidays, and after researching online and having discussions with several of her medical colleagues, it was decided that she had carpal tunnel syndrome. She had it once before, twenty five years ago.

By February the numbness persisted and a surgery was scheduled at Mayo Clinic. This surgery was done shortly after Valentine's Day, and the surgeon declared it successful. Even so, the numbness continued two...and then three weeks after surgery.

In the weeks following the surgery, she also began to notice a change in her gait as she walked. We discovered it in a very pronounced way one day while on a walk with McCail. She said, "Tim, I don't know what it is, but I'm convinced something is really wrong with me."

We decided to pursue an MRI of her neck and back, thinking that it may be a pinched nerve causing both problems. The neurological exam and results of the test led the doctor to conclude a second MRI was needed...this time a scan of her brain.

Both of us left that meeting terrified at the prospect of what this could mean, and we knew she had already failed several elements of the neurological test. Though the doctor assured us not to worry, we did not heed his counsel. Anxiety tore into our lives...again.

Anxiety is no respecter of persons or circumstances. At its core, anxiety is the result of having more than one thing to choose...more than one possible outcome, say, of a doctor's tests. The ripping of anxiety into our being is there because we are living between those two outcomes. When Jesus spoke of it, He called it "having two minds" or being "double minded," as James put it in his letter. Anxiety destabilizes everything, every thought, every moment. And we were now living in that foggy valley where nothing seemed clear.

At the end of the second MRI, performed just a few days after our initial neuro consult, the doctor called us immediately requesting we return to his office. We walked down the long third floor hallway of the Cannaday Building at Mayo Clinic in terrified silence. We were escorted immediately into his office, where he had already put the resulting images of the scan on his computer screen.

THE UNTHINKABLE

He turned the screen toward us, showing us an ominous bright image in the shaded background of my bride's skull. He said, slowly and deliberately, "I am looking at a three centimeter brain tumor. It's likely an advanced stage glioblastoma and, judging by the dead blood cells inside, it is aggressive and still growing rapidly."

Pam's face went blank. If someone had driven a tractor-trailer into the office and run over us, I would not have felt more stunned. She told me later that my face had turned perfectly, ashen white. I took her hand, now cold as we listened solemnly to the doctor we had met days before.

He continued, "I would have to say that, due to the sensitive areas where this growth is located, it is likely inoperable." Pam said slowly, "You mean it's going to kill me?" He lowered his gaze and then after an eternally long moment said, "I said I think it is inoperable. I'm not a tumor surgeon. But I wouldn't touch it." By then, we both were struggling to comprehend his words.

We were finished. With the appointment...with life as we

had known it up until that morning...and those last moments. He was an older doctor, and didn't know us but he did an amazing thing. He took one of Pam's hands, and one of mine and said, "Would you be comfortable with me offering to pray for you?" The floodgates of tears opened for both of us then, and he prayed a God-saturated and Heaven-sent prayer for us. I'm glad he did...in that moment I couldn't have found the words. His words, his comfort, and his prayer reminded me of my kind biology professor in college. I so wanted him to end with, "no matter what happens, the two of you are going to be happy." But I frankly didn't feel that in this moment.

Walking rapidly from his office to our car, half running from this horrible meeting, I wouldn't let myself think of what this could mean. I just wanted to pick her up, drive her home and pretend this whole day hadn't just happened. When she got in the car, we drove out of the parking lot. It was then our emotions swept over us like a tsunami and I could barely see to drive home for the flowing tears.

But after ten or fifteen minutes of weeping and crying out to God, a calm swept over both of us simultaneously. We began talking about how we were going to tell our children...our parents...our church family. And she began in that car ride home to plan her funeral service. "I want my funeral to honor God, Tim. You make sure that happens." And then, she began selecting music and telling me exactly what she wanted. To both of our surprise, before we got home in that thirty minute drive, we were able to laugh a couple of times. And my old biology professor's prophecy came to pass again... "No matter what happens in life, the two of you are going to be happy."

The morning we left for that fateful meeting was the last

morning I would feel "normal" as I had come to know it. It is a feeling, frankly, I haven't known since. When we returned home, the sun was shining, early spring was showing its colors, the air was warm...but nothing felt normal. It's amazing when your life has been turned on its head how everything around you continues...but you feel as though you are watching life...not living in it.

We moved through the motion of the next days, as Easter quickly approached, with a mixture of tears, memories, laughter, and vainly trying to come to grips with what was happening. We had reconciled to Pam's death, sooner rather than later. We spoke often and studied what the Bible said about healing...and about dying. We prayed and wept and prayed more.

But then, through a series of circumstances we believed only God could have orchestrated, we were called into an urgent meeting with a surgeon who had been with Mayo Clinic for six months. We learned this renowned surgeon had something of a reputation as a "miracle worker" in his own right, and he wanted to meet with us. Later we learned Hollywood is planning a movie about him.

His office called the Wednesday before Easter, urging us to come in that day...in an hour! We hurriedly complied and rushed to the Clinic and there we heard from his team what we wanted to hear...they wanted to attempt a surgery. Dr. Quinones, the neurosurgeon, called us at home that evening, and asked us to come for a pre-surgical consult on Good Friday, a sign we felt was a positive one. Her surgery was to be performed on the Monday following Easter.

It was during those days that I made a decision. It was not something I agonized over for long. As I began to realize the complexity of what we were facing, I also realized there was no way I could continue fully serving our church while offering her the care she would need following surgery. I felt it not as an obligation or simple responsibility. I felt called to care for my wife now, in the same depth of certainly that I felt when called to this church and our previous one or even to ministry initially. It came with clarity, certainty, and peace.

I shared this with our church body and leadership. I was prepared to do whatever it meant to take on her care as my ministry...and to leave the church I loved and had served for almost a quarter of a century. If I needed to retire from ministry altogether, that's what I would do. I didn't know at that time if we were looking at months of recovery, or the rest of our lives. The church graciously affirmed my new "calling," and promised their support in every way as I pursued it.

A BITTERSWEET EASTER

We left Easter Sunday's three services at Fruit Cove exhausted but also feeling uplifted by the church's love and abundant promises of prayerful support. They were as stunned by our news as we were, and I found myself saddened that once again, on this day of the celebration of resurrection joy, I had to bring news of crucifixion even as I had done on Easter of 1997 with the death of Nik and Ruth Ripken's son.

The role of faith and prayer in such a circumstance is inseparable from the pain and questions. We would know one thing in our heads and by faith, while feeling sometimes quite the opposite during the experience. This was certainly true for us in this time. We both would have periods of time when prayer seemed to be the furthest thing from our ability to attempt. Thankfully the times when this happened would seldom happen to both of us at once. I know there were times when Pam carried me...and others when I carried her. And I am also confident there were times when our wonderful church and family of faith

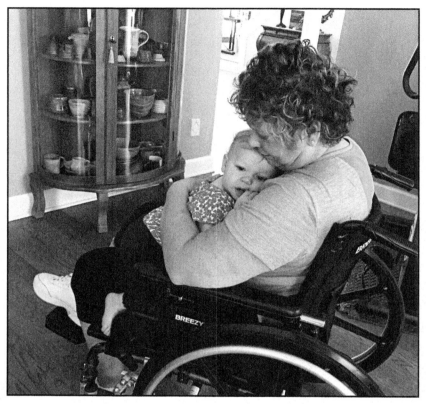

Granddaughter McCail was an inspiration for Pam during her illness.

carried both of us when neither of us could raise the banner of prayer for ourselves.

THE HIDING

E arly on Monday morning, following a mostly sleepless night, we arose and prepared for the trip to Mayo Clinic. Our daughter had come home to be with us over the weekend, and helped us get ready for our impending stay at the hospital. I was also planning to stay with her there.

Before we left, Pam went to her piano and played the last song she would ever play on this instrument she deeply loved and worshiped from many times a week. The piano was a gift of love I had gotten on our twenty-fifth anniversary...her ongoing gift to me was the blessing she was as she played it.

That morning, as she played a new arrangement of the hymn "He Hideth My Soul," I genuinely prayed for that soul-hiding to take place for her...and for me...that God would be our refuge and strength, a very present help in trouble. She had met God many times before in the previous months as she had begun to work on and worship to this song, and had planned to preview during a Lord's Supper service in the Easter season. This was not

The piano was always a place of solace for Pam.

exactly the way she had envisioned introducing it, but I believe today this may have been the most sincere moment of worship she had ever offered to God.

We prayed and sang praise choruses on the way to the hospital that morning. Allison offered her beautiful voice from the back seat. I honestly found it difficult to sing much...the notes catching in my throat...but I tried for her sake. We arrived at the clinic and I dropped my precious wife and our sweet daughter at the door while I parked the car, hurrying up to the fourth floor of the hospital as quickly as possible.

BEHIND THE CURTAIN

I was right to hurry. The nursing team was waiting for her to arrive, and since this was "her world" she received a royal welcome with doctors and nurses she worked with, people who genuinely love her, waiting now to care for her. They ushered her to the back, and I did not know as I watched her walking in with her colleagues, that this would be the last time I would ever see her walk on her own. Her surgical colleagues came and got me in a few minutes after she was settled into the holding area.

The residents and nurses had already come and drawn lines on her head to mark the area of surgical incision. This would be a hard procedure, lasting six hours with her awake for most of it. She was scared, and so was I as I sat and nervously held her hand, fighting every instinct in myself to just scream "NO" at the top of my lungs and take her back home...to deny this was even happening.

People came and went, some dressed in scrubs prepared for work and some in "civilian" clothing, preparing to go home or

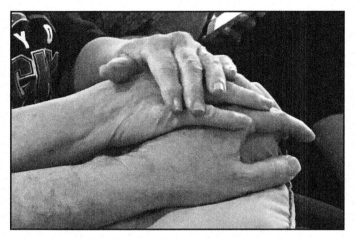

Tim and Pam's love deepened even as life seemed uncertain.

just arriving for their shift. Some, I could tell, came simply expressing sympathy, and a few out of curiosity. Some offered the promise of prayers...and some prayed there for us. Our Christian neurologist came in and prayed with us again. I wanted desperately to ask him, "Is this the right thing? Are we doing what we should in having this procedure?" I needed so desperately to talk to my dad...to have him tell me it's going to be OK.

I prayed over my sweetheart, my bride of almost forty years, lying so helplessly on the gurney. I was angry at myself that I could not just pray this away. I have had people tell me that after I prayed for them they got better...some were even healed completely. Why couldn't I do that for the most important person in my life? I hated myself in that moment, hated feeling so helpless in the face of this event, this trauma that threatened the life of my soulmate and my love. I would gladly have given my life for hers right then if that would mean she could walk away and be well and whole.

THE WAITING

Leaving that curtained room on the morning of April 17 was the longest walk I had ever taken. I was so thankful to exit the room into the loving arms of dozens of our church family and friends who had begun to assemble in the waiting room for the coming seige. It was so good having our children waiting with me. But my heart...my soul was in that room with Pam and would remain with her even though I could never know what happened that day.

I will never be able to find words to express how important it was to me...and to Pam and our children...to have the dozens of friends that soon turned to fifty and sixty gathered in the waiting room by day's end. We were constantly contacted by visits from her colleagues "behind the curtain" in surgery, who were keeping tabs on Pam's progress as best they could. The entire surgical suite was somber that day as the procedure continued, we were told by her operating room peers.

It ended at 2:00 p.m. As they had thought, the procedure took six and a half hours. She had done well through it. We were

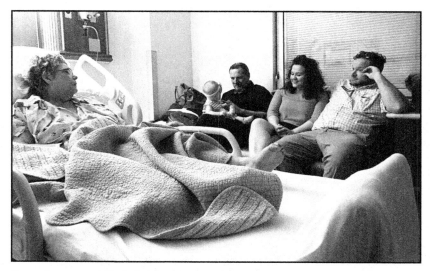

Dave, Logan and McCail visited Pam and Tim at the hospital, providing some relief and joy to some long days.

so relieved. The doctor met with our family and told us they had never seen a growth that looked exactly like this, and he was not even sure it was cancer. Only pathology could confirm what we were dealing with, giving us the first ray of hope we had felt on this journey. While much of the tumor remained, he felt optimistic about the outcome, and all of her functions seemed at that time to be intact. Hope sprang inside me!

THE OUTCOME

Two hours after surgery, however, a CAT scan confirmed what they feared could potentially be a complication...she had started bleeding into the cavity where part of the tumor had been removed, and a second surgery would be required to stop it. They took her immediately back into surgery, this time completely unconscious and under anesthesia. She had barely awakened from the first round of anesthesia. I was grateful she wouldn't have to endure another "awake" procedure, though I was very anxious about what was being done.

When the surgeon and his team entered the waiting room after two hours, at 8:30 p.m., we were unsure what to expect. We had already heard that they had managed to stop the bleeding; a call from the room an hour after they began had informed us of that.

They began with the good news: the tumor had now largely been removed, leaving only a small percentage of tissue behind. "But," the doctor cautioned, "we had to go deeper into the brain to stop the bleeding. We are unsure what we may have had to take to get to the area where the bleeding had occurred." I did not comprehend in that moment, through a mind numbed by the day's events, that his words carried an ominous tone. "What they had to take" may involve the permanent loss of vital functions like walking, and movement in her limbs, speech, even paralysis, as we later learned. "But," he ended, "she's alive and stable."

I guess in the moment that's really all I wanted to know. At the end of that hellish day, that seemed to be all that mattered. We still had her. The tumor was largely removed, though the cancer was still active elsewhere in her brain. The next days would more fully reveal the truth.

The ICU became our home for the next day and a half, as Pam would half-awaken and begin immediately to ask "nurse" questions. As I told her over and again, "You know too much." As nurses do. She'd seen a lot in her career, even though neurology was not her field. She knew too much about what could go wrong in some procedures. And she intuitively feared something may have.

The Mayo team was incredibly and wonderfully attentive to her...one of their own wounded soldiers. They moved us, earlier than planned, to a larger transitional care room to get us out of the spotlight and sporadic chaos of the ICU. I was grateful for the change, since I stayed in the room with her.

By Wednesday we learned that the initial in-house pathology did confirm a malignant tumor...news that was terribly hard to hear. It left us weeping late into the night. We had begun to hope against hope that she just had to recover from surgery and the nightmare may end.

It was on that same day we learned that we would have to go to inpatient rehab for her continuing recovery. While they were uncertain as to whether the nerve damage now affecting her right side was related to swelling from the surgery, damage done by the tumor, or injury caused by the second procedure, they said only time and rehabilitation would give us the answer.

Pastor Tim passionately leads his church in an appeal for prayer for Pam.

REHAB BEGINS

So Pam was released from Mayo and admitted to Brooks Rehabilitation hospital the next day. Due to her still-fragile condition, they had to move her by ambulance. I do not yet know why, and may never, but the days in the Brooks Hospital are some of my most difficult memories to face. The staff there was nothing if not kind and considerate toward us, and the therapists were excellent though, I believe, overwhelmed by Pam's situation.

Our first week, unfortunately, was nothing if not nightmarish. This was due not so much to where we were, but because of Pam's mental state at this early stage in her recovery. The days following her procedure created a great deal of swelling in her brain and a lot of confusion, due to the surgery and also to medication. She was given enormous doses of prednisone, and coupled with anti-seizure medications and anti-anxiety meds, it was chaos inside of her brain.

Several years ago, when she had fallen on her bike and broken her knee, I had to leave her in a rehab center that, in most

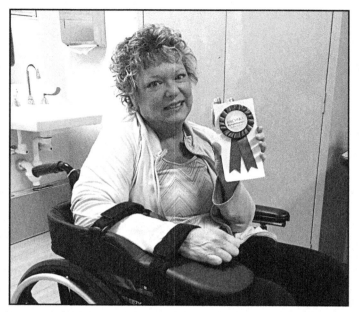

Pam, a nurse, was a blue-ribbon patient in dealing with her illness.

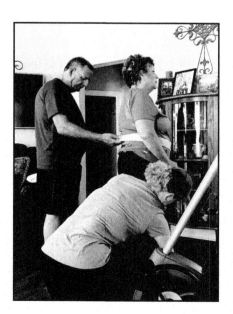

Tanya Klein was an invaluable friend during Pam's rehab. She is shown at left working with Pam.

Tim and Tanya worked together on Pam's rehab assignments at home.

every sense of the word, was nothing more than a nursing home. She shared a room with a much older and incontinent lady whose mind was gone. Her pain level was so great in those early days after surgery that they had sent her there with a personal pain pump to manage the therapy.

I would sit in my car after leaving her there night after night, sometimes angry and pounding the steering wheel of my car with my hand and sometimes broken and weeping over her situation. I promised myself I would never let her go through anything like that alone again. And so, I stayed with her each night at Brooks...listening to her breathing...waiting to hear her stir. She couldn't move the right side of her body much, and the confusion and early days of swelling and medication reduced her to helplessness.

I suppose, upon reflection, that this early stage of her recovery and her reaction to the interaction of the medications at work inside of her caused me to spiral into as close a state of despair as I have ever known. I could do nothing...NOTHING...to make this better for her. I prayed and wept by her bedside, and seldom left the room, at least in the beginning. Allison stayed with us through much of the first week, relieving me greatly, and Dave and Logan and McCail visited at every opportunity they could as well. The baby's visit was the only thing that made her smile but we decided we really didn't want McCail around this setting much.

Printed instructions on her door and over her bed stated in large letters: "CANNOT RESPOND TO MULTIPLE STAGE INSTRUCTIONS." Her aphasia and mental trauma would not allow her to process commands we would think of as simple, such as: "Press the button...call for the nurse." That would involve TWO commands. I could not leave her in a room overnight when she was not even able to call for help if she needed it. Several friends and members of our family asked, "Why don't you go home?" My response was simple. "She is my home."

Update on Pam - April 26

Beloved Church Family,

We are so appreciative, again, for the countless offers of help and your unceasing prayers on our behalf. We thank God constantly for you. Believe me your prayer matters!

It has been difficult to write sometimes because we are still in the early stages of absorbing exactly what we are dealing with and what recovery is going to look like. We know that time and effort, and the healing grace of God will help recover what has been injured in surgery.

In the meantime we are fully in the rehab process at Brooks. Pam is doing well and making progress according to our team. We are both weary as would be expected... and sometimes discouraged. "But we do not lose heart." Our timeline to return home is Friday week.

We miss being with you, our church family, very much and eagerly look forward to our return. Hopefully I will be back in the pulpit Mother's Day.

Our therapy team has asked us to limit contact with visits for a while longer as we continue to assess Pam's condition. Some symptoms will subside when swelling does and some medications are discontinued.

Others we will have to wait and see. We have been assured by her physician that most of the effects caused by surgery will be resolved within three months.

We also are awaiting outcome of final pathology from Mayo and that certainly is a matter of prayer.

Many, MANY have asked "what can we do?" and certainly prayer is the first response. But in a week or so we will return home and need our family... YOU... to stand with us in the next steps forward.

You are an amazing and caring church body. We could not imagine going into this trial without you! Thank you for loving us, praying for us and standing with us as we continue to seek honor and glory for our Savior even in this.

He is a good, good Father.

Pastor Tim and Pam

THE DARKNESS FALLS

In that time, I realized she was also in her own personal sense of despair. I didn't know how deep it was. On more than one occasion in the first five days, she begged me to pray that she would just die. I told her that was a prayer, first of all, that God would not answer. And secondly, I would not pray that as her husband or as her pastor. She said more than once, "If you love me, you'll pray this will end quickly for me. You cannot want me to live like this."

I understood. There were moments when I wanted to just close my eyes, and go home and be with Jesus, too. I have never before or since felt that much darkness and despair, even in grief, within myself. And we talked a lot about how sweet that time will be, and one day that time will come, when it will all be over and we'll be together with Jesus in Heaven, and never again be apart, but we don't want to give up yet.

By the end of week one, we had begun to learn how to get her up and out of bed and into the wheelchair or into the bathroom, but the requirements of therapy were more than she

Pam's ordeal was both mentally and physically exhausting for both of them.

could manage. I learned as much as I could, and got "approved" to move her without calling for an assistant. But I could not do the required therapies for her.

When the team came in for our first end-of-week evaluation, we simply said, "She cannot do these therapies. Send us home. Let someone have the room that will get value from it." We were both exhausted, and facing more time in this place was beyond our physical, mental, and emotional endurance.

We called our children and told them we were just going to go home, and do whatever rehab we could do from there. That evening was the first time that I was parented by my kids. David and Logan came that evening, gave us a few sweet moments with McCail, and then firmly but respectfully gave us a piece of their minds. They read us the riot act about quitting and giving up. I truly have not been so firmly handled since the last time my dad did it when I still lived at home. I had never seen my son so passionate...almost angry to the point of tears...before.

And so, hat in hand, I went that evening to the neurologist handling our case at Brooks and told him we had changed our mind and would like to continue inpatient rehab if that was still possible. He said it was, and made the changes necessary for her treatment to continue there.

Update – May 2

Beloved Church Family and Praying Christian Community,

Today has been a day begun with disappointment and ending with some difficulty but along the way the hand of God is still guiding. This we know. Our plan, we thought, was to go home this morning. Immediate modifications had been made to our front door with a ramp, and a newly renovated shower to accommodate Pam's immediate need for a wheelchair. Great friends in our church saw to that.

Our bags were packed and sitting by the door when the doctor came to visit our room and shared with us his belief that, given the progress Pam had made so far, a few more days of intensive therapy in Brooks would be very advantageous to her recovery. With some disappointment, we agreed that, if a few more days here would help, we are in.

A few years ago a popular Christian tune stated that changing one letter in the word "disappointment" then became HIS appointment. We believe that to be true.

So we changed the letter and buckled in for another week.

It was a blessing and encouragement over the weekend to have family visit from Ohio as Pam's little sister came to see us with her husband. Pam's mom, Shirley was released from the hospital in Ashland which was a great relief. I even found out late yesterday that the sofa I have been sleeping on since we have been here was brand new! I'm the first to break it in. Thankful that it hasn't broken me.

Last night we watched the Celebration of Joy service via livestream and the message of finding joy, not happiness, zeroed in on our hearts. We wept as God broke us by speaking right into our room through Dr Kinchen.

Along the way, other blessings have come in the form of a helping friend who has "adopted" us and made herself constantly available to work with Pam when the therapists here are not. And then, though not actualized yet, there's the "meal train."

As the day unfolded some of our newfound enthusiasm in the hopeful report from the doctor was tempered as Pam had a recurring migraine that actually appeared first at 8:30 on Sunday and has continued in clusters throughout the day. It has been a painful experience for her especially since the normal meds they use wasn't resolving them. The origin is still a mystery to everyone but God.

However, as the Sovereign and loving hand of our good, good Father continues to orchestrate events, we learned that our doctor here is one of the leading specialists in the country in migraine treatment! He has researched and written numerous journal articles. If we had gone home and this had happened, it would have been awful.

I write this in the darkness of our hospital room as Pam at last is sleeping comfortably, and I am remaining awake to pray for her. It was then I learned that hundreds of believers have joined in this part of the battle to pray. We are simply beseeching the Lord for the pain to subside and rest to overtake her through the night. It has overwhelmed me to see the Christ followers across the nation and the world take part in this battle... and I truly do not know how to say thank you enough.

We have seen throughout the day how God turns disappointment into His appointment. Maybe you're there right now... sitting in the darkness wondering what is happening in your life... your tears... your disappointment.

I trust that you will join me as we wait and see what God is up to... sometimes in our joy, and other times in our tears and fears. He has a plan... an "appointment" for you. Trust Him in it. We are seeking to hang on to what we know of God's character and love... even if His appointment may seem to you right now to be disappointment. He won't fail you. He will not let you go. Ever.

With great love,
Pastor Tim

THE STRUGGLE
FOR RECOVERY

We stayed in the unit on the neuro floor at Brooks Hospital on University Boulevard a total of three weeks and three days. Pam fought so very hard, believing that the more rehab she did, the more quickly her speech and thought processes would return to normal...her feeling would return to her hand...and her ability to walk would be restored. No one could have been more determined than she was to will this to happen.

She was nothing if not persistent. She never backed down from a challenge. It was both encouraging to see her take small steps forward, and heart-wrenching to see how far she still had to go. We encouraged her and cheered her on, in spite of seeing with our own eyes the long distance she had to travel. The surgery, while necessary, had markedly and, I was beginning to fear, permanently reduced her capacity to think, to speak, to process emotion, to walk, to use her hand...in short, to be herself.

A Word from Pastor Tim – May 8

Sometimes, in the midst of our sorrow and pain, we forget that we are not the only ones hurting. Wednesday night, following the pathology report for my wife revealing the level of her brain cancer, I desperately needed some time to just walk and think... and pray. So I took some time to go and circle the parking lot of Brooks hospital where we have been in recovery since Pam's surgery.

As I walked outside, the last thing I wanted was a conversation... with anyone. But as I left through the sliding glass door of the hospital, there stood a man I had walked past many times over the past several days as he pushed a brain injured young lady in a wheelchair and safety helmet. He was a stereotypical redneck; baseball cap, beard, jeans. I had spoken to him many times like guys do... you know, deep stuff. "Hey bud." "How's it going?" Or just a silent nod. I saw him heating up a McDonald's sandwich in the microwave one night for his daughter, and offered him some leftovers from a meal my daughter-in-law, Logan had made that night for us.

But that evening I didn't want to hardly make eye contact. But I did, and said, "How's it going?" And he started telling me about his daughter, crippled for life by a road rage incident with her boyfriend. They were leaving in the morning and heading back to Rome, Georgia. They had been here two months. I wished him well and wrapped myself up in my pain again.

As I walked away God landed on me like a load of

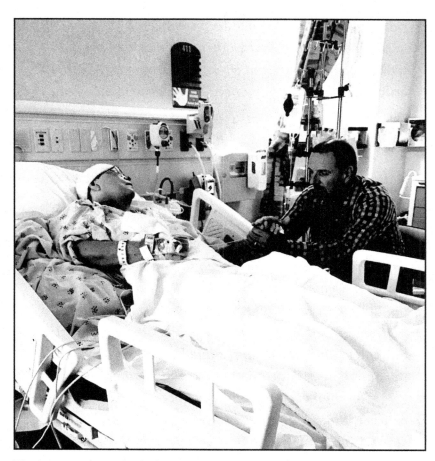

Tim kept a constant bedside vigil with Pam following surgery.

rocks. There was my opportunity to offer comfort, attention or even a prayer for another hurting human being. A man who loved his daughter and who my Father loved.

I continued walking under the load of conviction, promising God I'd get up early next morning to pray for the guy. But that didn't cut it. I kept trying to walk away from that still, small, piercing voice inside of me. And as I circled back around the parking lot, I saw him again... sitting alone, smoking a cigarette.

So I approached him this time. And I got honest with him. I knelt down and said, "Hey man, my name is Tim. My wife is here recovering from brain surgery. I'm a pastor and I was just so lost in my own stuff a minute ago. I'd like to pray for your daughter and for you if I may. And I'd like to tell you that there is a God who loves you... and her."

He said, "That would be really great. Thank you."
So as I knelt beside him, I prayed for Jerry and his daughter Shannon. And I walked away with my load a little lighter, and a reminder that I serve a God who wouldn't walk past my pain.

Even as He hung on a cross.

I think it was while lying awake in the room during one of the endless nights and walking with her in the hallway at Brooks that I began to see and accept the truth...that I was going to lose my wife. Maybe in the days before the surgery and a couple of weeks after it, I was in denial that these things were going to be permanent— but now began to see that she may not recover completely...if much at all.

The neurology team at Brooks wanted to know how I was doing. I told them a few years ago I was rear ended by a semi that had his load shift. I remember the impact seemed to take 15 minutes as everything went in slow motion. I saw stuff flying around me like it was in a gravity free chamber. That's what this feels like. Everybody else is moving in real time; I'm in slow motion. Life is frozen

Pam agreed with that assessment. The experience in the weeks following Pam's diagnosis, surgery and then three weeks in rehab has seemed timeless. We have a big clock on the wall in our room. It has meant nothing.

When you get rear-ended by an experience you never saw coming you suddenly see everything that you had neatly in place go flying in pieces. That experience happens in many ways to people.

It is unavoidable. But even in the midst of the chaos and uncertainty of that experience there can be a constant to anchor you: the peace of Jesus

Today I walked into the Brooks lobby after getting a clean shirt from my car. As I stepped in there was piano music. It was so nice I stopped because I didn't know there was a piano there. And then even more amazing "It is Well" was the song playing!

I looked up onto the mezzanine and saw a therapist standing by the pianist. Then I looked closer.

Pam was playing the piano! The therapist was assisting but she was playing along with her left hand and it was amazing... and just at the right moment God showed up...

... again.

"My peace I give to you...." Jesus

A couple of months after Pam died, I made a hospital visit to a church member in Memorial Hospital next door to the rehab center. It was my first time back there since our discharge. All of the memories of those dark days came flooding back, and I realized it would be healthy for me to take some time to drive to the parking lot where I had spent three of the most painful weeks of my life.

The tears began immediately as I saw the winding path where I would push her on evening walks in the wheelchair. I drove past the prayer garden, with a jasmine-covered arch where we sat and prayed, enjoying the fragrance of the flowers in April. I looked over the water where rails were placed so that she could pull herself upright from the wheelchair, pretending for a few brief moments that she was normal as she stood. I began to debate where these rails could be installed in our house.

After ten or more minutes of outright anguished tears, the emotion shifted quickly and I acknowledged my anger for the first time. I was angry. Not at Brooks hospital. They were nothing but wonderful for the most part. Maybe at the surgeon? Maybe at the circumstance?

Maybe that we did so much, suffered so much there for nothing? Maybe that they all but promised us in writing that she would be able to walk out with a cane and she couldn't? In the moment I could not distinguish the target of my anger...but it was real and came as ferociously as the hot tears that flowed in the previous moments.

I will confess some of my animosity was directed at having to be in rehab at all. While many patients who were undergoing brain surgery were informed to expect rehabilitation as a normal course, this information was never shared with us. In fact, when Pam packed her bag for the hospital, she selected workout clothing to recover so she wouldn't have to lie in a robe or gown.

I drove away after a time of remembering, still not knowing why the anger came with such a force in those moments. It continues to arise from time-to-time...not with daily frequency, but it doesn't lay far below the surface. I am assured in literature I have read and by counselors with whom I have met with that anger is not an unexpected response, but surely it was not one I am accustomed to experiencing.

Beloved Church Family and Praying Friends,

Today we learned from Pam's surgeon both good news and bad news. The good news was that God was gracious in the surgery and 99% of the tumor was removed in two surgeries. The bad news was that pathology showed the mass was a Grade 4 Glioma. This will require consideration of further treatment through chemotherapy and radiation. Next week, we will meet with the oncology team at Mayo to hear what they want to do. We will prayerfully hear their approach and seek God's wisdom about our next steps.

We are "knocked down but not knocked out," to quote Paul. It was discouraging to hear the pathology outcome, but we are ending our day encouraged about steps forward. "Therefore we do not lose heart." We know that it is in our weakness that God's strength is made perfect. We know that our God is able to do impossible things; even heal cancer.

We ask that you continue interceding as we continue another week of rehab, leaving on Mother's Day weekend. Please pray that Pam will continue to improve as she has already impressed the team here with her resolve and progress. She has already heard one team member say that they had never seen anyone do as well as she has done in such a short time! We will press on, believing God for His power to work on our behalf.

We have a good, good Father who has never let us go! You have shown us His love through your many acts of kindness through cards, thoughtful gifts, food and so many, many prayers! We are grateful beyond words for each of you.

With our love,
Pastor Tim and Pam

In our last week at Brooks we went to a followup visit and consult with the oncology team at Mayo Clinic. We were met in the exam room by our surgeon, Dr "Q," and his team of residents and associates. They filled the small consult room, and surrounded us as we sat together with Pam in a wheelchair and me on the sofa. They sat on the exam table, a few stood, and one of the residents went to the desk to turn on the computer screen and call up images of the "before" and "after" of the surgery.

As cheerfully as they could, they told us the good news that the tumor was virtually gone, at least beyond the point we could see it. But they also delivered the blow that the tumor was still active in other areas of her brain that could not be seen on the screen. The tumor they had encountered had an insidious name: astrocytoma. One of the assistants described it as "the beast." Seemed appropriate.

Defined, this growth was star-shaped with tentacles that reached into various areas of the brain. For us, it was also known as the same tumor that had taken my father from me fifteen years before. The battle, he warned, (and we had already begun to realize), was far from over.

Pam had already made up her mind that she was not willing to undergo radiation or chemotherapy unless it was absolutely certain it would improve her condition. She told the doctor and his team as much. Her energy and resolve and lack of progress at Brooks had truly disheartened her...and me. Neither of us at that time had much fight left in us. She just decided that she didn't have the energy to continue fighting with the added burden of radiation and medication that would further weaken her in the effort to continue rehab.

The medical team was insistent that, with the outcome of a positive surgery and the advances in therapy and radiation available that her life expectancy could be prolonged. They prevailed on us until we finally agreed to at least make a visit to the oncology and radiation appointment for a conversation. We agreed and then left, but did so with a sense that they had already seen that her prognosis was not a positive one, even with added therapy. Their efforts to persuade us, though well-intentioned, were not entirely effective.

An Update from Pastor Tim – May 13

Today we come home! Our journey from surgery through in-patient rehab is now complete. We rejoice to come back to our house since we have been away now for four weeks. It seems as though we have been in a foreign land... or on another planet.

While we rejoice greatly in the strides Pam has made in rehab, we still have some distance to travel. The neurological deficits on her right side are still affecting her and will until the swelling from the surgery subsides. In the meantime, we will continue to persevere in rehab as outpatient.

Next week we will also visit again with Mayo Clinic to determine the next steps in treatment of the remaining cancer which, again thankfully, is only 1% of the tumor. We are hopeful about the treatment going forward.

God did a miracle in Pam's life, of this we are certain. Recently we learned that the second surgery she underwent was an emergency surgery that they thought might take her life. God worked a second miracle that day to spare her.

But God's miracles are not half-way. We believe that He is not only going to heal her of this cancer but

He is also going to restore the function to her body that has been impacted by the swelling following surgery. We are grateful that her memory, her intellect and her comprehension have not been affected by this, though each are located in the area where her surgery took place. We are told the issue with speech she is facing is temporary and will respond to rehab.

You have been amazing... simply beyond words amazing... in your encouragement for us, your prayerful intercession on our behalf, your care for us in food, emails, texts and Facebook posts and your faith in God for her healing from this disease. Please know that your ministry to and love for us is felt, appreciated and needed as we move forward.

We cannot thank God enough for a church family like you... and for the great things He has done and will continue to do through you. Please continue to pray as we walk through this journey in the days ahead trusting our God who is able to do more than we could ask or expect. He alone is worthy.

Tim and Pam at home for the first time after rehabilitation following surgery.

COMING HOME

We had our homecoming from the hospitalization the weekend of our fortieth anniversary. This was the year we were going to take a long- promised and long-postponed cruise to Alaska. We had promised ourselves each year that, when we arrived at our fortieth, we would take time to truly celebrate what God had done in our lives. But this was not the celebration we had anticipated by any stretch of imagination. However, we were relieved and grateful to be in our home, and Pam wept profusely when she saw the place she had lovingly decorated and arranged and cleaned and cared for and made "our home" still waiting for her there.

I pushed her in the wheelchair through the house she had lovingly decorated, lived in, and dreamed about. She lovingly ran her hands over cherished items accumulated over the years. We went into the back yard, courtesy of wooden ramps to accommodate her wheelchair, and she saw the plants that, unfortunately, had been often neglected over the past weeks . The swimming pool we had remodeled just the previous summer finally had some finishing touches completed while she was hospitalized. She wept when we went through this "world" she had created for us to enjoy in retirement, both of us silently knowing but not saying that it may not be one she would get to enjoy for long.

Adjustments to the house began immediately...some already undertaken. Our shower doors and compartment had been taken down to allow us to wheel her in. A great friend made ramps for our porch and front door.

Tanya Klein showed up at Brooks the week after Allison left and, as she had done some years before when Pam was recovering from a broken knee, came in and assumed much of Pam's care. She didn't need an introduction to our house. It was good that she came when she did. I was virtually paralyzed and completedly overwhelmed. Pam did not want a "stranger" coming into our home to care for her, even though insurance allowed for visiting nurses. Tanya reminded us time after time, "I'm all in" despite our protests. And she was. And together we promised Pam through all of this, if at all possible, that no one would be seeing to her care but us.

With Thanksgiving – July 28
"Come into His Presence with thanksgiving...."
Psalm 95:2

I heard this week from someone that gratitude is the key that unlocks the blessing that God wants to give His children. In times of trial and difficulty, it becomes too easy to overlook the simple expression of heartfelt gratitude that needs to be spoken and heard. This is, for the moment, the best vehicle I have for getting that gratitude delivered.

It is absolutely overwhelming for us to experience the blessing and generosity of Fruit Cove Baptist Church. While the greatest gift you have and are giving us is the gift of understanding my need to be away from my duties while Pam is ill, so many other gifts come with that. I am grateful for a staff team and willing to step up and step out in support, prayer, encouragement, and in the fulfilling of extra responsibilities while I am away.

I am grateful time after time for warm and thoughtfully prepared (and delivered) meals each day. Overwhelmingly so, if I am not overusing that word. We have been the recipients of countless gifts of flowers and fruit and gift baskets and gift cards. We have, again, lost count of the greeting cards and thoughtful statements posted though Facebook and text.

But let me circle back again. I am grateful to you... each of you... and to you as a body for giving me the freedom and incredible gift of time with Pam in these hard days. You are an amazing congregation and "I thank my God on every remembrance of you."

So blessed and privileged to be your pastor. Pam and I love you so very much!

We spent the money we had saved for a cruise on a new mattress that would automatically raise and adjust to allow us to get Pam easily in and out of bed. We didn't want a hospital bed, since I wanted to be able to sleep beside her at night for as long as possible. So Tanya and I improvised a railing system that would both keep her safe at night and help her pull up in the bed when needed. Other furniture was moved around or out of the house to allow us to move her wheelchair with ease.

A Word from Pastor Tim – May 18

We are home. It is good... and also hard to come back to familiar surroundings but to find that, though things remain the same, much of our life hasn't. We are still dealing with several realities on a daily basis, specifically concerning the absence of feeling in Pam's right side including her arm and leg, hand and foot. Her speech continues to return rapidly and we are grateful. And we continue on in outpatient therapy to learn to accommodate these problems created by swelling in the area where surgery took place. It is uncertain how long the swelling will create pressure on the nerve center in her brain that controls her right side.

And so we wait. We pray. We press on through exhaustion, medication and sometimes discouragement. "But we do not lose heart." We believe and trust still that God is going to do an amazing thing in our lives through this. Please pray that God will soon allow feeling to return to her right arm, hand, fingers, foot and leg.

Each week we have been in this trial God has given us a word. Not a verse. Not a passage. A literal word to hang onto. The first week, the word was "persevere." The second week, it was "restore." This week, the word has been "mercies." Don't ask me how I know. He doesn't text it. He doesn't always even "light up" a Bible verse. But He confirms it. Sometimes in a conversation or a card that someone has sent, sometimes in a song we are listening to or an email or even from a book we are reading, He gives us the word. That's often all we can handle... a word. But it's an important word. A hopeful word. A word of life.

Let me say again what I have often said before. You, our church family, have been nothing short of incredible to us. Your contacts and touches, lovingly prepared meals and gifts sent to our home, your cards (Pam has now gone through over 60 and we still have a huge stack), your gift cards, your concern expressed in ways large and small have been a literal... LITERAL... oasis in this wilderness experience. We have always sought, when someone gives us a gift small or large, to try and write a note of thanks somehow. We are far beyond an ability to ever do that... to ever adequately say thanks. We are actually overwhelmed by the avalanche of blessings. But please know we are so very, very grateful for each one! God is showing, through your love, that He is a good, good Father.

And so we look for mercies. We ask for the mercy of quick and miraculous recovery from this trial and for Pam's restoration. We see the "new mercies" of God at every turn. Even yesterday when I accidentally did a "California roll" through a stop sign in one of our communities, a young deputy stopped me in his patrol car to remind me that we are not in California and that

in Florida, stop means stop. He took my license, brought
it back to me after a few minutes and said, "I'm letting
you off with a warning." Mercy.

We serve a God who has promised us that, each
morning, we will see new mercies. I hope and pray for
all of us that our eyes can be opened to appreciate each
one that comes! "Because of the LORD's great love we
are not consumed, for His compassions are new every
morning; great is Your faithfulness." (Lamentation 3:22-
23)

Grace, mercy, and peace...

Pastor Tim and Pam

And just like that, we were "home." But things were far
from normal. Rehab continued several days a week formally
through the outpatient center at Brooks as we could schedule
appointments. Since Tanya had attended each of the inpatient
sessions at the facility with Pam, we continued many of the same
therapies that did not require specialized equipment at home as
much as possible.

I think of all the difficult things we endured through those
weeks and months, the most trying for us was working with Pam's
limited mobility. This seemed to frustrate her more than the
speech limitations and perhaps more than even the loss or use of
her hand. The idea of having to exist in a wheelchair was
something she never came to accept. Fighting her mental
resistance to this circumstance was an ongoing daily battle.

Each day, whether through specialized equipment at the
rehab center, or through our makeshift "rehab" facility into which

we had turned our house, we labored to help Pam recover her mobility. We were told that the idea was to retrain her brain... translate "teach her to walk again." The tumor and surgery had obliterated her brain's memory of using her right leg. Moving it artificially was supposed to "rewire" her brain reminding it how to use the immobile limb.

Using a gait belt for safety and a specialized cane, we would help her to stand using the leg and foot she couldn't feel. Then, painstakingly, she would take a halting step with her left leg, and with me stabilizing her, Tanya would crawl along beside her moving her right foot, placing it on the floor where it would give her the most balance. Then Pam would "catch up" with her left foot and the process continued.

Day after day, we took each step, hoping with each one that something would "connect" the damaged wiring so that she could move without two people assisting. It never happened. But to Pam's credit, though we could see her deep frustration, her determination to make this work outweighed it. I saw again what my wife, my soulmate, was made of in this experience. I doubt I would have worked as hard with as little result. But she kept her hope that her ability to move would return at any time. Each day we prayed fervently that it would.

At the same time, we were chasing outpatient clinics all over Jacksonville trying to get Pam in to see neurological specialists which, we learned, were at a premium. Further, she seemed to improve little through the appointments to her, and our disappointment. Pam fought so hard in those final months to seek to recover what she could of her physical functions that the cancer and surgery had taken. Slowly, however, we began to realize that these functions were showing no signs of improvement and in fact had begun to decline again.

Adding a layer of great difficulty through all of this was the visit we finally were able to schedule with the radiology department at Mayo. We had prayed much and talked long about the option of chemo and radiation, and even though we knew that the prognosis with both was not great (the surgical team thought it may only give us twelve to fourteen months of life), we prayerfully decided to start the treatments.

That morning as we sat in the waiting area, we had agreed to come back as soon as possible, even the next Monday to undertake the "mapping" MRI to allow radiation to begin. And then, we were invited back to the small waiting area where, again, Pam waited in her wheelchair and I on the sofa by the doctor's desk.

The radiation oncologist came in, a kind young female doctor, and after a few formalities informed us that due to the absence of two DNA markers in the pathology of the tumor, chemotherapy would not be in any way effective in slowing or stopping its growth. The medication is designed to "bond" to the malignant cells and kill them. Pam's pathology would not permit this bonding to take place. Radiation, she informed us, would simply serve to burn out areas of her brain making her permanently lose cognitive function, memory, and further limiting and permanently reducing mobility.

For the second time, the truck ran over us. We sat stunned by her words. And we asked out loud the question lingering in the back of both of our minds. If we don't do anything else, how long can we expect Pam to live? Her response, "three to six months." With the full course of treatment that we were expecting to undergo, she guessed maybe twelve months or possibly a year and a half...but with significant decline in quality of life. We told her we would trust the good hand of our gracious God to bring the healing she needs.

So we left the office at Mayo Clinic that day. This would be Pam's last visit there as a patient or as a nurse. We left the property that day in silence...and spoke little on the drive home. Our minds were spinning with so many questions that neither of us wanted to speak aloud.

A Word from Pastor Tim – May 22

In the 1990s, the contemporary Christian music scene was dominated by one voice and one name... Don Moen. Don was on the "cutting edge" of revolutionary Christian music. Today, he would be considered "classic" or even "traditional" by some. Although his music is not on the front burner of churches now, one of his songs still resonates with many people. The song is "God Will Make a Way." The chorus says:

"God will make a way, when there seems to be no way.

He works in ways we cannot see, He will make a way for me."

I loved that song when it came out, and still find myself singing it sometimes in heart and spirit when tempted to grow discouraged. Today, I believe these words more than ever.

Pam and I are living each moment believing that

God is going to make a way in our circumstance and experience. We believe He has "made a way" in providing us with a surgery that has removed 99 percent of the tumor... an incredible result. We believe He is going to make a way as we continue.

Last week, we decided after meeting with Mayo's team that radiation and chemotherapy would not be pursued as an option in the treatment follow-up. But we still believe that God will make a way. We have asked God for a miracle in her circumstance... and many of you have joined us in that prayer and intercession. We believe by faith that He is making a way for this to happen... in ways we cannot see! "Without faith it is impossible to please God." "But with God all things are possible." We are trusting Him for that.

We still have many residual issues to confront as we go forward. Pam is still experiencing a loss of function in her right arm and hand, leg and foot and other issues following the surgery. It has severely limited her ability to walk and to use her right hand. We believe these issues will respond to rehabilitation but it will take some time and a lot of hard work. PLEASE PRAY that she will be able to walk and use her right hand again quickly!

We love you, our church family and praying friends, for continuing to lift us up in this journey. In many respects, it has been a wilderness experience and yet we have never sensed God nearer. He has sent us a caring "angel" to help us through in the person of Tanya

Klein. We are incredibly grateful to her and to many others... our wonderful church staff team; the hundreds of cards, texts, emails, gifts of food delivered to us by you and help around our house and yard. We are literally overwhelmed by the outpouring of love and concern even from folks we don't know!

And His presence has never left us, even though we have had some dark nights and hard experiences. Your constant encouragement and prayers for us has been a lifeline to the Father's throne. PLEASE CONTINUE TO PRAY that God's story will be written large in our experience for His glory and honor.

The song continues:

"He will be my guide; hold me closely to His side
With love and strength for each new day, He will make a way."

Living for Christ alone,
Pastor Tim and Pam

EVEN IF

I t was through this time that I began to finally accept
we were waging a losing battle. During one outpatient
appointment as I dropped Pam with Tanya and went
to park the car, I glanced through my email on my phone for a
moment. Allison had posted a song on Facebook by MercyMe
that morning titled "Even If." It was as though the Lord said to
me through that song, "If I don't heal Pam, will you continue to
praise Me?" Through tears for the first time, I faced that reality
head-on. And through those same tears, I once and for all said
"yes."

During this time, after several deep conversations, we
decided to reach out to Hospice to help us with some specialized
medication Pam needed. Her anxiety was worsening...an
expected symptom that comes with the brain processing
something of this magnitude. Along with that, depression is also
a common side effect and I was uncomfortable trying to secure
and administer the meds without a doctor or nurse to oversee it.

Earlier we had discussed calling Hospice to do an

assessment and get paperwork completed, knowing at some point they would be needed. Pam had even brought it up at breakfast. Later that day, I called for an appointment and told her in the afternoon they would be coming the following week. But with that news she broke down in tears and said, "Why do we have to do it right now?" I canceled the appointment.

This time she was in complete agreement that they needed to become involved. In each step of her treatment from surgery to the pills she took each day, I respected the fact that she was the "medical professional" in the room. This was a source of comfort to her, I believe, and one of the last things she could feel in control of in her life. So I continued to follow her lead as long as she could express what she wanted.

But now, it was time for Hospice to come.

A Word from Pastor Tim – May 26, 2017

I am praying for a miracle.

I struggle, as many in our tribe do, with the subject of miracles and faith... healing and prayer. How exactly are we to think about such things? Does talking and thinking about them... believing in them... actually make us Pentecostal? Throw us in the camp with "faith healers" and carnival hawkers? Is it fear or sophistication that stops us?

Or is there a place for them in a consistent biblical theology? Living as we do in a culture immersed in naturalism (the worldview that says nothing true exists beyond the things that we can immediately experience with our five senses), it is easy to keep our collective mouths shut when the subject of miracles comes up. We may secretly believe they happen but to talk too much about it calls our sanity into question... at least for some.

I am praying for a miracle right now. Even as I write this blog, it is part thinking out loud but mostly prayer and shoring up my own faith. I believe I have seen miracles in the past. Not just the "miracle" of a beautiful sunset or watching my granddaughter learn to walk. Those are incredible things that happen, but few of us really think about them as "miraculous." But I have seen genuine miracles in people's lives... and believe God still does them.

I am praying for a genuine, bonafide, certifiable, quantifiable and unquestionable intervention from the Father who "knit us together in our mother's womb." I am asking for our Sovereign Creator who is also our Father to interrupt natural processes AGAINST the normal ebb and flow of everyday life; against the normal outcomes; against the data that science provides; against the impact of cancer in Pam's body and its impact as it threatens to take so much.

I am praying for a Moses -standing -on- the- beach- at- the- Red Sea- parting of waters. For a Joshua "fit"- the- battle- of- Jericho- wall collapse. For a Jesus walking on water and raising Lazarus kind of miracle. Of taking God's Word in simple faith that we can "ask whatever we will and it will be done for you" and beg for His interruption of growth of cancer cells and the loss of function that occurs after such surgeries.

A rare photo that includes the family of seven with Tim and Pam, Patrick and Allison, Dave, Logan and McCail.

The day of McCail's first birthday party was bittersweet. Pam learned that morning her father had passed away.

I am praying for a miracle. For the glory of God but for the sake of my wife I am praying that God will step in and do something amazing. And I'd like to ask you to join me if you will, asking... without doubting... that our God not only is able... but that God wants to "show off" His power to a skeptical world. Sometimes we are guilty of making God too small to handle the really tough stuff. Maybe He is ready to be magnified and not minimized. Maybe we need to "tap out" and turn Him loose on our big stuff.

All He asks for is faith. Not believing for the sake of believing. But faith... trust... dependence... leaning into His arms and letting go. Trusting a good, good Father who longs to step in if we'll just ask Him and Him alone.

I am praying for a miracle. And who knows?

Maybe, you're in need of one too!

THE EVERLASTING ARMS

Reaching the point of accepting that she could no longer participate meaningfully in rehab at Brooks and ultimately at home was a difficult turning point for her. We ultimately had to stop attending church, which was also heartbreaking for us both. Now that Hospice had become involved in her care, and as part of their policy they permit no outside resource other than what they provide. Rehabilitative services were not an option and our visits to Brooks had to come to an end...and our journey to acceptance of the last stages of the dying process began in earnest.

We had hoped, we had prayed, we had believed, we continually read Scripture and books on miracles; we prayed some more with hundreds or maybe thousands of other people. But God said no, and the song replayed in my mind..."even if." "Though He slay me, yet will I trust Him," Job had said. Can I do that...could we? Even if God doesn't deliver as we have prayed... will we praise Him still?

Our faith had never been tested in a furnace this hot. We

had always had a medical "option" to fall back on, but now we didn't have a doctor or a medical recourse. We had stopped calling the Mayo oncology team since no course of recovery was offered to us. Our surgeon's office had stopped calling us. They had all reached their conclusion...the cancer was terminal. The answer was not in their hands or their abilities. We were thrown completely in the arms of God, which thankfully are "everlasting arms" beneath us. And He proved to us that He is enough...as we had earlier claimed...and that He could hold us though we were broken beyond repair.

A Word from Pastor Tim – June 28,

A year ago on June 27, a little bundle of beauty and joy exploded into our world. McCail Violet Maynard tipped our world upside down and we became grandparents! It's a learning curve to be sure and much different from parenting in many ways. This lil grandarlin' of mine is a heart-stealer. It isn't her smile with a couple of new teeth or the moment she lays her head on my chest for a moment and sticks her thumb in her mouth, she has totally absorbed me. McCail has filled our lives with blessing. She's "talking" now. (Well... she knows what she's saying anyway.) She is, after all, a girl.

And I could never say enough of how proud I am of her Mom and Dad. Dave and Logan have become THE most incredible parents raising my granddaughter to be pleasant, happy, lovely, good-natured and socially well-adjusted. She can also bust a mean dance move when her "jam" is on! She is reputed to be the favorite at her

daycare... no big surprise there (sorry other kids). And I am living for the day that my little sweetheart looks up at me and says, "I love you Poppy"
PS. Mamaw loves you too!

It was now June. We had never thought or expected that we would attend McCail's first birthday party with Pam wheelchair-bound and recuperating from brain surgery two months earlier. Our whole world now revolved around her care and what we hoped...that healing would still come. In spite of medical reports to the contrary, we continued asking that God would still heal her miraculously.

But in spite of the grim prognosis, Pam continued to fight. She wanted to give this battle all she had for me and for her children. She wanted to see her granddaughter grow up. Our goal had now been reduced from seeing her walk freely to simply asking God that she might be able to get out of the wheelchair and go into the bathroom without assistance. But in all of this, she suffered well and overflowed with grace.

I have formally studied three languages. I have taught and tutored Greek, dabbled some in Hebrew, and spend my lifetime reading, speaking and writing in the English language. But I can find absolutely no words to express how painful it was to watch my bride, my wife, my love go through those last months of her life. We did not want to admit to each other the truth that both of us knew. She wasn't going to come out of this. Death was coming.

A Word from Pastor Tim – June 23
SOUL ANCHORS

A few years ago, I was allowed the privilege of doing a visit aboard the USS Enterprise (CVN 65) off the eastern US coast. We were flown aboard while the ship was underway, and tailhooked onto the deck alongside dozens of fighter jets, helicopters and scurrying sailors.

During our tour we were taken into a large, aft, holding area. There, in this cavernous room, we were shown an amazing thing... the anchor chain and mechanism that could secure and hold an aircraft carrier. Each of the chain's links was man-sized and able to secure a 100,000 ton vessel in a churning sea. Impressive anchor.

And yet, there is one more impressive than that. It is the anchor that holds our souls secure in the rolling seas of uncertainty, suffering and seasons of darkness. Hebrews 6:19 calls this anchor "hope." "We have this hope as an anchor for our souls, firm and secure."

Hope secures us in times of uncertainty. I read a recent study that shows American anxiety levels are now at a record high and have risen sharply since 2014. We are anxious about terrorism, identity theft, natural calamity, disease, finances and war.

Many have no anchor... no hope. While many of us tend to think the cross was the earliest visual symbol of faith in Christ, historians tell us we are incorrect. The earliest symbol was an anchor.

In the time of storm and stress we are personally walking through right now, both Pam and I can testify to you: the anchor holds. It is secure. Our anchor holds.

Hope is what we hold to in the struggle.
And we know that as we do, the Father always
holds on to us.

Things intensified for the worse the Saturday morning of McCail's first birthday party. At 9:00 a.m. we received a call from Pam's sister Debbie that their father had passed away that morning. Though 92 years of age, he was not unhealthy and his death was totally unexpected.

I thought I would not see deeper pain in Pam's beautiful blue eyes before the news of her father's death, but when she heard these words a door shut inside of her. She was fully crushed by the hearing of this news. I do not honestly believe she ever recovered.

That day, I gave up. I surrendered. The family was gathered around the phone in the living room. Pam sat weeping in her wheelchair, ready to go to the birthday party. And I walked out, slammed the bedroom door and fell on my knees at the foot of our bed. And I resigned. For the first time, I really and truly gave up. I told God, "I quit."

I had tried desperately, feverishly to walk through this experience keeping my attitude as well as Pam's where it needed to be. For over forty years I had looked out for Pam...protected and provided for her and prayed for her. That's what husbands do, and I embraced it...never resented it. But this was now too much. It felt to me that God had now turned His back, or at best become an absent and silent friend. By faith I knew that He wasn't any of those things, but I felt what I felt. What was I supposed to do with this news of her father's death? We couldn't travel...she couldn't fly with a brain tumor even though in coming hours we received two separate and amazingly generous offers to fly her home in a private jet. I hit my lowest point then. I felt trapped by a circumstance I couldn't control, and instead of throwing me a life preserver, I felt, in the midst of this storm, I had just had a large hole torn in my liferaft.

A Hard Place and the Rock – August 2

Idioms are commonplace in the English language and in most others. They are easy to remember phrases and sayings, catchy in their presentation, and express a reality that is commonplace to humanity. "Six of one and half dozen of the other." "Raining cats and dogs." "What doesn't kill you makes you stronger." (My friend Nik Ripken sent me a photo of a plaque he found in a store on barn wood which was a commentary on the last statement. The plaque read, "I don't know if this is killing me or making me stronger.")

"Between a rock and a hard place." This is not a hopeful idiom. It conveys a sense of doom, of helplessness, of being trapped with no way out. It was how Aron Ralston felt when he found himself trapped with his hand beneath a boulder during a climbing accident. His "way out" was to amputate his forearm with a knife and no anesthesia, graphically described in his autobiography Between a Rock and a Hard Place.

It describes the position of the Israelites trapped between the sea and the onslaught of Pharaohs terminators coming to finish them off. The only way out was through trust in God. So they trusted and God made a way. The ROCK came through for them and the sea parted, drowning Pharaoh's army in its return. God seems to show up in these impossible scenarios!

Paul knew about the hard places and the Rock. His resume is colored by experiences in the pit of despair, peril, disease, persecution, spiritual attack, false accusation, injustice, imprisonment and physical limitation. He should be the patron saint of every person who suffers, because he has pretty much been through it all!

He spoke of this in the inspired writing of his letter to the Corinthian church. In 2 Corinthians 4, he speaks of being "hard pressed on every side." In other words, he was "between a rock and a hard place." He gives us clear insight on how to process times in the hard places. His counsel has been, if you would, "road-tested."

As I read his testimony, I find it bracketed by the words, "therefore we do not lose heart." (4:1, 4:16). What's the key to surviving the "hard places" of life? Don't lose heart. Don't give up. Don't give in. Don't quit. Cling tenaciously to your faith. God is clinging tenaciously to you, and has promised us that "As your days so shall your strength be..." and "underneath are the everlasting arms." (Deuteronomy 33:27)

We have an unshakeable bedrock beneath us as we stand on the ROCK... as we build our lives on that foundation, and not the "sinking sand" of our own strength. An elderly, African-American preacher would remind his small congregation each week of a massive truth. He would say, "Brothers and sisters, I often tremble upon the rock, but the rock never trembles under me."

You may be in that place today, that hard place, where you find yourself "trembling upon the rock." But I know you will find, as we have, that the rock never trembles under us. "And you can take that to the bank!"

During the season since Pam's death, I came in contact with an author and fellow struggler who is also a pastor. He, too, watched his wife go through the travail of brain cancer, and he wrote honestly of their excruciating twenty-year experience. It challenged his faith on deep levels as well. He wrote in one part of his book entitled "Losing Susan" that he was looking for a bumper sticker that said, "God loves you...run for your life." In that dark moment, I understood his sentiment. But I know that our God will not allow Himself to be easily understood. He is too vast for that...too far beyond us. His ways are higher than our ways. His thoughts are higher than our thoughts. His paths are not always easy to understand, or to walk on. And He will not allow us to manipulate Him...only to trust Him.

This is so important to remember, especially when the heavens seem locked in silence. The doorway to God's throne is never closed, and yet at times it seems as though it may be not only closed, but as C.S. Lewis colorfully put it, "slammed shut and bolted" against us.

It is then, he further reminds us, that our walk of faith is truly being tested. When no obvious sign of God seems to exist, when the joyful feelings are no longer part of our emotional system, and when it seems no evidence of God even exists, and we still reach up to the Father...our faith is the real thing and Heaven rejoices. We will find it tested this way on occasion.

A Word from Pastor Tim – July 12

I find myself again needing to express the sense of gratitude that Pam and I feel for the continual stream of encouragement and the caring gifts of food, gift cards, and most of all, prayers from our beloved Fruit Cove family for Pam's recovery.

We are literally overwhelmed each day knowing the body of Christ is reaching out to us and ministering in ways both visible and invisible. Knowing that prayerful vigils, thoughtful emails, cards and Facebook posts and wonderful meals are being offered to ease our journey in the wilderness of this experience brings grace in ways that you cannot imagine without experiencing it.

And we certainly could not fathom going through this trial without knowing that a faithful, church family is standing with us and kneeling before the Father continually carrying our burden to Him. Though our journeys out are becoming more and more difficult our hearts join yours in worship to our good, good Father as Fruit Cove gathers on Sunday. We worship and weep with you in praise to our Heavenly Father and Healer.

We are learning each day to look to God for our daily need, knowing that He promises renewed strength for each day as we trust Him to provide. Daily we are leaning deeper into Him, and know that "underneath are the everlasting arms."

From devotional writer Andrew Murray, we are learning four anchor points to secure us:

1. *We are here by His purpose.*
2. *We are here under His care.*
3. *We are here for our training.*
4. *We are here until His timing is fulfilled.*

So we walk by faith and trust His heart and His provision and His purpose. Long ago we surrendered our lives to Him and gave ourselves completely to His control. We continue to do so.

And He has never, ever let us down.

I knew that God loved me...and Pam...and her dad. But God will not allow us to easily pin Him down with shallow platitudes and simple thoughts. He does not let us lock Him in the box of our own understanding, shutting Him in where we can keep Him safe and tame and controlled. The cry of Jesus from the cross, "My God, my God why have you forsaken Me" shatters any idea we might have that God is easy to understand.

I do not pretend yet to understand or explain how Pam's experience through all of this was an affirmation of that love. I felt forsaken and I found renewed faith almost in the same moment at times. I can find "good" things that came about afterward and even during the journey. But to say I always knew with great confidence of His love in some of those days would be a stretch...and dishonest. My head knew it, and my theology affirmed it. But my heart was broken and I was emotionally and spiritually shattered as I watched my wife be crushed by this disease and now, adding to our sorrow, her father's death.

We "attended" her dad's funeral in our home church via Facebook Live, courtesy of my brother Mark's iPhone. Our pastor and friends, Glen and Susan Owens, came and sat in the living room with us as the service took place. It was a fitting celebration of Leonard Sloas' life as a husband, father, grandfather, veteran and Christian. He loved Pam so very much, and I truly believe her illness hastened his death. I believe his heart was literally broken over it.

In my memory, his death marked a clear decline for Pam both cognitively and physically. It was not long before she began sleeping more and more and more. We tried waking her to keep her in something of a routine, but gave that up eventually. She began to decline in her diet and fluid intake. All of these, Hospice informed us, were signs of her body beginning to shut down. We knew it could be weeks or days. I knew this was so.

The last three weeks before her death, she slept almost constantly...14, then 16, then 18 or more hours a day. Her waking hours were disorienting, and even without drugs that made her sleep, she couldn't stay awake. We tried watching TV, and as long as she was conscious we read our devotions together and prayed before she went to bed. After she had begun sleeping round the clock, I continued reading Scripture over her. I did so every night whether she was awake or asleep. We had both known and believed that hearing was the last thing to go. I trust that is true. And I knew that building her faith was the only thing I could try and do now. "Though our outer man is perishing," Paul wrote,"yet our inner man is being renewed day by day."

A Word from Pastor Tim

Sunday, June 4, is Pentecost Sunday. That doesn't mean much to most evangelical, Protestant types, according to a journal article I read recently. We don't really acknowledge the special dates on the church yearly calendar (well, except for the fun ones... Easter and Christmas with an occasional mention of Advent.)

The church calendar is built around several, significant observations and celebrations and observances, much as you will find reading the Old Testament (Feast of Passover, Day of Atonement, Feast of Booths, etc.) They literally controlled time and worship for entire communities of earlier Christians.

Lent is a 40-day commemoration of the 40-year, wilderness experience. It is followed by a 50 day "Hallelujah Party" following Holy Week and Easter Sunday. Then, at the end of the 50 days, Pentecost Sunday arrives. It is the birthday of the church. It is the day the Spirit of God fell on 120 praying men and women in an upper room in Jerusalem, tarrying for power from on high as Jesus had commanded. (Acts 2)

Pentecost became a day of salvation, of fulfillment of prophecy, of the powerless disciples being clothed with power from on high as a "mighty, rushing wind" came and literally took over their lives. The Holy Spirit had arrived... the Presence of Jesus in His followers. The Promise had been fulfilled!

But this year, Pentecost Sunday has taken on special significance for me. It is 50 days from Pam's surgery. Her surgery was literally 7 hours after Easter had ended. We have wandered in the wilderness of surgical recovery and rehabilitation and emotional discouragement and disappointments and physical exhaustion and weeping... waiting, as did the disciples, powerless but prayerful; empty but expectant.

I believe God is going to do something on Pentecost Sunday to endue with power and fresh anointing, restoration of strength to Pam's leg and dexterity to her hand and arm. I believe that this God whose name is Yahweh (Jehovah) Rapha is indeed the "Lord who heals us." That this God who parted the waters for Israel will do the impossible and bring healing to a disease that doctors have said can't be cured.

On Pentecost Sunday, I am praying He will be that for Pam. I am not demanding. God is Sovereign and He is under no obligation to answer any demands. "God is God in Heaven and does whatever He will." I am not ordering. Nor do I believe myself to be presumptuous or naive.

I simply believe He is a good, good Father who is going to show Himself in power. So I ask: Will you pray for Pam? Would you pray on Pentecost Sunday in a special way for her? Will you pray that God will show Himself in power for His Own glory? Would you pray for the power and Holy Spirit unleashed at Pentecost to visit her?

And may God hear the pleas of His people,
rend the heavens and come down!
I waited patiently for the Lord and He turned to
me and heard my cry for help. He brought me up from a
desolate pit, out of the muddy clay, and set my feet on a
rock, making my steps secure. He put a new song in my
mouth, a hymn of praise to my God. Many will see and
fear and put their trust in the Lord. Psalm 40:1-3

So many things tear us in different directions in this kind of circumstance. I was torn between praying for a miracle and trying to reconcile what I saw happening in her body's decline. Hospice counselors and others advised us to "prepare for the worst but hope for the best." But that counsel is destined to keep human emotions in a constant state of turmoil.

I would hear medical professionals state what they knew to be the case...she was not going to survive this. At the same time, I felt within my heart and spirit a voice calling me to pray one more time...to believe. To have faith in God. To not give up or give in.

It was a constant battle to find the right words to speak to her, and I didn't always choose well. I wanted to encourage her to believe, to think positively. Yet she knew, as I knew, what the prognosis really meant. She would listen patiently to me, thinking, I believe, that the things I was saying to her were helping me more. So she'd let me say them, even though she had moved past them already.

We tried to keep up a brave front for our children, and Pam would never let a visit with Dave and Logan and McCail go by unless she had made some effort to dress, apply makeup, and fix her hair. I think it was not until our last meal at the kitchen table with her that it truly hit my son how bad this really had become, as we watched her struggle to put food in her mouth from her plate.

It was during that visit where she struggled simply to eat that McCail took her first steps with a little walking toy we had gotten her for Christmas. I am grateful to God that Pam got to watch, and laugh, and enjoy seeing her granddaughter take her very first steps. "She's walking at lot better than me," she joked. But I did not miss the sadness in her voice.

An Update from Allie Martin – July 24, 2017

Dear friends and family,

We had a great time visiting this weekend with Mom and Dad. Patrick and I came home on Thursday and surprised them with our visit! Mom was so happy to see us! We were able to have a nice family dinner Thursday night with Mom, Dad, Dave, Logan and McCail too! McCail showed off and walked by herself for the first time! We were so glad Mom was able to witness that! Friday evening we had dinner with Mom, Dad, Tanya, me and Patrick, as Dave and Logan headed to Tampa for their anniversary trip! We got to be there to say goodnight and tuck mom into bed Friday night, and that time was very special! I plan to come home again very soon!! I wanted to share an update on mom since we haven't posted one in a while...

Mom has been sleeping a total of 17-19 hours per

day the last 2 weeks. It is very hard for her to stay awake most of the time, and Dad and Tanya are doing all they can do to keep her comfortable, which in the last week has included calling in-home hospice. We are planning on keeping Mom home and assistance from Hospice will allow us to do this. They will be assisting with whatever is needed to keep her home. Mom's appetite has decreased and it is becoming harder and harder to get her to eat well. (Especially with her sleeping as much as she has been) However, with us home this weekend, she was up a little bit more and ate more than normal, which is great. By the way.. We continue to appreciate everyone who is helping with meals! You have no idea how much it helps Dad and Tanya caring for mom everyday not having to worry about meals!! Thank you so much to everyone who has and continues to help there! Mom's mobility has continued to decrease, and her left side has become affected as well as her right side, which has made rehab impossible, and we have stopped rehab completely at this time. Her speech is affected and her aphasia is increased to the point that there are times where we cannot understand what she is saying. Her pain levels are minimal right now, but she does complain of her right arm hurting and her head hurting-basically a dull, constant pressure-type pain from the tumor. For now, they are able to manage her pain with medications.

Mom is not able to be on Facebook at this time, but wanted me to thank everyone for praying for her and loving on her (and us) during this time! She said she loves you all! We know that God is Good, and He will bring healing to my mother. It's looking more and more like her healing will soon be in heaven. Please continue to pray for my mom and the family at this time as we try to support her and keep her as comfortable as possible.

Also, if possible, please refrain from texts/emails/phone calls to Dad and Tanya as they are focused on caring for Mom full time. We will continue to update through the Facebook group and church emails. Thank you for continuing to love our family! We feel the prayers and know our strength is supported in those prayers!! God is good all the time... and we want our song of praise to be "It is well".

Allie Martin, daughter of Pastor Tim and Pam

I was constantly torn over what to write; what to post online. How best to inform a loving and waiting church which eagerly wanted to be informed to better know how to pray was a constant struggle. Pam was determined to project a "positive" image to those who watched us walk through this valley. While we wished at times to suffer in private, our family and friends and church needed to join us in this. We were "wounded healers" walking through this experience. So in this time we began the "Pray for Pam" Facebook page to help inform and keep those who were walking with us and praying for us posted on where we were. Our daughter shaped much of that for us.

One of the more painful dimensions of this journey was having to go through so much of it without people near us. This was not Pam's desire, or mine or, for that matter, but theirs. When

I had surgery for cancer a few years ago, I was adamant with Pam that I didn't want people around me during or after the procedure. I only realized later how hard that was on her. She had told me that, though she reluctantly honored my request, it made her experience so much harder, and forced her to walk through it largely alone.

I thought of that often as we had to turn down request after request for a visit with her in our home from people we deeply loved. Her mental and emotional state was often such that a visit would usually send her into an emotional downward spiral, or even raise her level of anxiety. The doctor theorized that the tumor was affecting a part of her brain's ability to process emotion normally, and when she was on anti-seizure medication this effect was intensified. Sadly, the very thing that should have and could have helped her and encouraged her in her healing had become a liability that we had to curtail. Short of our immediate family, we had little contact with those outside our household during those months.

PART 6

ENDINGS

The Deep

Most of us have vivid memory of the first time we stepped out of shallow water into the deep. That moment of sheer exhilaration and magical weightlessness that comes is followed by sheer panic and fear as a mouth-nose-lungful of water floods in! It may have been an accidental foray or a swimming lesson; going from the wading side of a pool past the rope that marks the deep end. Or perhaps it was a lake, the creek or salty, ocean water when your feet suddenly could not feel the stability of the bottom.

Maybe you were aware enough to fight to keep yourself afloat in that moment. In all likelihood, a rescuing hand reached out to save you from the water. Once on vacation when our kids were smaller, Dave (then about 5 or 6) decided in enthusiasm to jump into the swimming pool at the motel where we were staying. He chose the deep end. Sank like a rock. In panic, I jumped in after him... clothes, shoes, wallet and all... to grab his hand and pull him to safety.

Today may be for you (as it is for us) a time of "doing business with God in the deep." (Psalm 107:23-24) Maybe it is a time of helpless or hopeless sinking, and you find yourself struggling to breath. The waves seem to get higher and the bottom farther away. And you await the rescuing hand of God.

He is coming. Your Savior knows where you are today. Though your circumstances may be washing over you like huge ocean waves... though stability provided by your own strength seems a thing of the past... your Deliverer sees you and is coming.

God receives the greatest glory in the "deep." If we spent our lives wading shallow creeks or kiddie pools, we would see and know little of the glory of God because we feel that we are sufficient and our strength is enough. There is no need to trust. But as we cry out to Him in those times in the depths of life, we will find how small is our strength and how great is our God. We find that we are not forsaken or abandoned. And we find our deliverance will be accomplished...but not in our strength or by our own ability...

...only by His.

TIL DEATH DO US PART

The end came almost exactly as the Hospice personnel had projected as they would monitor her vital signs each visit. We had started giving a small dose of morphine in her final week, which was the first drug that we gave to address her pain beyond Tylenol and Advil. Ironically, the only complaint she ever had was with her right arm as some sensation began to return. Tanya had massaged it for more hours than I can remember, trying to help her manage the pain. But it hurt her constantly and intensely. Other than that and a chronic low-grade headache, her pain seemed to be minimal and was usually manageable.

In Pam's last days and hours, she spoke very little. I'm not sure how much she really knew of what was going on, and I know there were times off and on some days when she didn't know me.

She did have one amazing moment when, I am convinced, she was allowed a glimpse of heaven. She had said little for some time. We had thought she might not speak again. She was sitting up in the bed for medication and to try and drink some water. We had been praying together and talking to her, and suddenly...as though her eyes were opened...she said, "I see my Daddy! Uncle Franklin!" (Her Mom's brother who had just died months before). And then, in a broken voice, she began singing "It is well, it is well with my soul!" We all wept together for the joy we felt in that moment. It truly helped prepare us for her homegoing.

These were among the last words she spoke that we clearly understood. Allison had come back home earlier to be with us and she and her mom had some precious last moments together, saying only things moms and daughters can whisper and understand. She had arranged family leave from her job to be with us during Pam's last days.

I was honestly at a point of physical and mental exhaustion by then and the last days are a blur to me, and still are even months later as I have tried to sort them out. I do not remember the sequence of events clearly; days and nights blurred together. We even removed the wall clock since time had no meaning to us anymore.

It was early on Friday evening, August 4, that her breathing began to be more ragged and shallow. She had become unconscious by then, never to awaken again. Her breathing became labored, then ragged, and then sporadic.

Early on August 5, her breathing stopped and she opened her eyes in Heaven —leaving the tears, and pain, and medicine, and cancer lying in the bed with her battle-weary and now lifeless body. We were gathered around her in the bedroom those last hours. Death had indeed parted us physically, but certainly our love continues because "love never fails."

The battle was now over for Pam. The words "it is finished" that Jesus spoke from His cross took on new meaning to me. And now she was home... "though absent from the body...she was present with the Lord." She saw Jesus...her father...my father. She had lived her life well. She had loved me and our children well. She loved and served her Savior well. And when her race was over, she died well.

In the hours immediately following Pam's death, a variety of emotions struck almost simultaneously. Tears flowed in abundance. We turned as quickly as we could together to songs of praise. I asked Allison to play, "Bless the Lord, O My Soul," one of Pam's favorite songs. We also listened at my request to the MercyMe song I had mentioned earlier entitled "Even If."

You've been faithful, You've been good
All of my days
Jesus I will cling to You
Come what may
Cause I know You're able
I know You can.

Certainly we prayed. We gave thanks that, in this moment, we had hope...not despair. We reminded ourselves that "to be absent from the body was to be present with the Lord." That Pam had "run the race, fought the good fight, and kept the faith." She had finished her course well. She now wears the "crown of righteousness," promised to all who love Jesus and faithfully await His appearing. Pam was in that number.

After a time, we began the harder work of calling Hospice to come and then of informing other family and friends that Pam had died. Allison agreed to apply makeup for her Mom's beautiful face, no longer in pain from the struggle of her battle. She truly looked lovely and serene after Allison finished. And then we waited for the nurse to come and complete the task.

Allison, Tanya and I were exhausted beyond reason by this time. We were thankful that Pam now had entered rest...so richly deserved. But we learned the moments and hours following a death are anything but restful for the survivors.

Tears continued to flow...tears of sorrow, of loss, and of relief. Thankfully much of the emotional work of preparing an obituary notice and of planning the funeral service had already been completed. All that remained was making the necessary calls for these things to be put into action.

We decided that the service would be planned for Tuesday and to do so in the evening, with limited time for viewing and visitation since we knew the crowd would be enormous. This was out of concern for me...and Pam's mom. We wanted maximum convenience for family and for friends who wanted to be present. This decision was one of the very few that Pam did not plan for the service.

She had asked me some months before if I would do the service when she died, and after she saw the look on my face she retracted her request. "Let's ask Glen to do it." Glen Owens was a good friend whom we had requested to be our pastor through this time. I struggled doing this, simply because I was not only Pam's husband; I was her pastor. The only one she had known since 1982. The one she had left home and family to follow for forty years of life and ministry together. While it would have been my greatest honor, I also knew at the time that my mental and emotional state would not permit me to do it.

Dave, Allison, and I went the next day to make arrangements with the funeral home. They were incredibly gracious and accommodating to us. I had worked with the director dozens of times in the past few years, and was actually the first pastor she had done a funeral with in Jacksonville. She cleared her schedule to oversee this service at my request.

I sat in her office with grieving families more times than I could remember. But it's a different experience when you are the one expected to answer the questions. Again, much was already prearranged, but several items still had to be finalized. I also had some personal requests about items I wanted included in the casket with her body; among those a blanket that she had clung to for comfort through many days and nights. She had been a blanket baby, and I often teased her that she had never outgrown it.

Pam made me promise that there would not be a viewing. I honored that request, though I knew it would be better for some — maybe for me — if her body could be seen. However, she had been hesitant to allow this because she knew the impact that cancer has on appearance and the body. So to ease her mind I promised that there would be none, though everything in me wanted to see her once again and touch her face and hair. That is something reserved yet for the future, when the tears and crying and cancer and heartache are gone. I greatly look forward to it.

GOING HOME AND THE REALITY OF HOPEFUL GRIEF

I learned that it is a hard thing to grieve as a husband and, at the same time, pastor the loving congregation who wept and prayed and bled along with us in this journey. I now had to process, not only my own grief and my family's, but also to speak into the grief of the church family now shaken by the news of Pam's passing — a church that had loved and served us so faithfully through these days. I felt their grief acutely. Hundreds of cards and email posts had expressed their concern, along with numerous times cars had simply parked in front of our house to pray.

My son-in-law Patrick, a senior pastor in Alabama, blogged a note from us, and Allison posted information on our "Pray for Pam" Facebook page which she had begun and largely maintained for us through this time. Again I am grateful for their handling of this since words were not coming together for me in this season... spoken or written ones.

I've been sitting here drinking Tim's coffee this morning. If you've never had a cup of "Tim's coffee," it's a... well, it's an experience. It's the consistency of motor oil, and it's nearly as strong as it is thick. So, the concentrated caffeine always gets me to thinking, which isn't something I need help with much these days.

I've been thinking much of Pam and how grateful I am to her for providing me with (next to Jesus) the single greatest treasure of my life in Allison. I've reflected on her legacy, which I see in the faces of family members as they walk by me and my inordinately strong cup of coffee. McCail just walked by and it reminded me of how, even in the last weeks, that little girl made Pam's face light up. This house, and all the quilts, stained glass, tiffany lamps, and beaded and tasseled lampshades, reminds me so much of her. And that's okay... the memories I see here are all good ones that I'd like to hang onto.

I've also been thinking about all of you. It's easy in our situation to get somewhat closed off from the rest of the functioning world. You've been so good to bring food, cards, flowers, etc. You all have been more of a blessing to our family than we could ever have hoped for. But, regardless of your location: 50 states, 7 countries, multiple continents, etc., you've been so good to pray for us. You've "Prayed For Pam" for so long, and you've been so good to send all of us texts, emails, and even the occasional "snail mail" to show us your love. There have been times when we couldn't respond right then, but please know that we've felt every one.

But, now it's our turn... we know you've been praying for us. But, we want you to know that we're praying for YOU! We're especially praying for our Fruit Cove family. This is a unique situation for you in that your shepherd is walking through the grief process right alongside of you. We're so grateful for Neal Cordle and the rest of the staff family at FCBC, as they've been walking alongside you. I believe that God brought each one to Jacksonville specifically for this purpose, among others. But, as a family, we wanted you to know that while we haven't always been able to express it, we've been praying for you just as much as you've been praying for us.

The church is a family, and family takes care of one another and lifts one another up. We want you to know how much we love and appreciate you for holding us up these last few months, and we want you to know that when we pray, we pray for you, too.

Thank you for being family to us.

Patrick Martin

Our staff and ministry team were absolutely wonderful to us in helping coordinate a large funeral service on our campus. Our deacons stepped in to provide a meal for my family before the service which was so appreciated by my family, though I remember eating little.

I came to the church campus that evening with my family, in a fog of tears and grief. I was allowed some moments alone at the casket containing the body of my beloved before the service began. Pam had chosen music for the service, but we chose music to play beneath the pictures that Allison and Dave had assembled. An instrumental piano worship CD recorded by Pam a decade before played in a constant loop as the pictures rolled (almost an hour's worth with NO repeats). Again I'm so grateful Allison handled this task as well.

The sanctuary was quickly filled with a long line of well-wishers and friends who came simply to "sit" with us through this service. I have long advocated the "ministry of presence" to our ministry staff. This period of my life proved again the importance of such ministry. Showing up...not with the right words, or wise words, or comforting words...but just showing up is so vital. People struggled to know what to say to their pastor. I was supposed to be the one speaking words of comfort to them.

That night, it was estimated nearly 1,400 people were in attendance in our sanctuary and overflow area. Over twenty-five hundred log-ins were recorded via Livestream. We heard later of several churches, including our home church in Catlettsburg and our first pastorate in Shepherdsville, that had gathered people to the sanctuary and broadcast the service there. Missionaries around the world had logged in as well. One couple rose in the middle of the night in their part of the world to watch and to be a part of her funeral.

It was decided to leave the organ vacant for the service. We decided it best not to use it, and instead to drape it in lovely red roses on her bench where she had invested more hours in rehearsals and worship than could be calculated or estimated on earth. But I know God kept a record of every one.

The service began with a video that was made the morning

of Pam's surgery...the last time she would play this instrument she loved so much. Allison secretly caught it on her phone. It could not have been a more wonderful gift to have, especially knowing now it would be the last time she would play it. As she began in the dim light playing a few bars of the song, our pianist Kathy Lane picked up the arrangement and opened the service with the hymn "He Hideth My Soul." I sat in tears reflecting on the scores of times Pam had filled our home with beautiful piano music over the years.

Neal Cordle, executive pastor at Fruit Cove, welcomed the congregation with comments and prayer, and then the orchestra played "Great is Thy Faithfulness," the song Pam had requested they play for her service. Several orchestra members visibly wept as they played.

Jason Lovins, who had "adopted" Pam as his "Florida Mom," and Brian Woofter, our worship leader and our worship choir offered incredible vocal music. Dr. Peter Murray of the Mayo Clinic, one of the last doctors Pam would work with as a surgical nurse, agreed to speak about her in her professional role. He did an amazing job of honoring Pam as a Christian nurse, and her colleagues present echoed their deep respect for her professionally.

I was amazed at how many people, both there in the service and for weeks afterward, contacted me to tell me how much Pam had meant to them both as friend and mentor. She had influenced countless young women to go into or stay in the nursing field, or to serve at Mayo Clinic. And her testimony as a believer was clear to all who knew her. She had stood her ground and lived what she believed...and was deeply respected for her

A photo of Pam sits on the organ during her memorial services at
Fruit Cove Baptist Church.

Pam playing the organ at Fruit Cove Baptist Church that she enjoyed so much.

Pam's funeral was a true celebration of a life well lived.

testimony.

After more full-voiced and heartfelt singing of praise to the Father, including Pam's favorite hymn "Come Thou Fount of Every Blessing," Patrick stood to speak. He read and commented on a piece written by our friend Carolyn Nichols to recommend Pam as the recipient of an annual Pastor's Wife award given at the Florida Baptist Convention each year. Her words were so fitting, and were energized by Patrick's personality and comments.

He stayed on the platform as he introduced me next. I didn't know whether I could make it through a speaking role in the service or not. And so, I wrote my words down in detail for him to read if I could not. These words are included at the end of this chapter. As I spoke, a strength came to me that I did not have a moment before. It was the same strength God gave me to speak at my father's funeral fifteen years earlier. It could only have come from God. At Pam's service and at my dad's, I was sitting in a pool of tears just before time to speak. And then, the peace of God visited and flooded my soul.

I felt it was important for me to stand and, at least for a few moments, attempt to minister not only to my flesh and blood family but also to my spiritual household. They were hurting so badly, and my heart was torn for them...and for myself...and for my children...and for Pam's mother and sisters. And by God's grace, I got through all the remarks. And most of all, it was my privilege and important for me as her husband and her pastor, to bear witness to the faithfulness of a godly woman, a loving spouse, an incredible mother, and a head-over-heels in love grandmother to McCail.

My Eulogy for Pam

My son-in-law Patrick will be "lurking" behind me as I try to get through this. I have written out my comments so he can step up and finish for me if I can't. I don't know how to do this. You may not know this, but Pam and I would usually "slip away My son-in-law Patrick will be "lurking" behind me as I try to get through this. I have written out my comments so he can step up and finish for me if I can't. I don't know how to do this. You may not know this, but Pam and I would usually "slip away" between services for a few moments where I would steal a kiss a get a...."review" of the sermon. She would either come in with a few enthusiastic comments about it, or she would change the subject to "where do you want to go to lunch today" or "your tie was crooked" and tactfully avoid telling me what she thought. I don't know who can tell me today. You know it's hard being the wife of a pastor. If you know one today tell them how much you love them. Their man could not do what he does without them. They have to be not only a public supporter of their spouse...but also the one who knows him best. It's hard to let a person be your husband...and your preacher. So if she liked what I said, I knew it was good. I knew I wasn't being hypocritical in what I said. She was the one to tell me. I don't know who can do that now.

I read 2 Corinthians 4:6-8 to the church this past Easter morning as we were lessthan 24 hours from Pam's surgery. We have read it and drawn strength *from it many times since.*

It has been said that marriage is the act of bearing witness to another person's life. One other person receives the gift of seeing you live out your life on the deepest of levels. Forty years ago on May 14, Pam and I said "I do" on a makeshift altar in the side yard of the Oakland Avenue Baptist Church in Catlettsburg, Ky. Our relationship began two years earlier when I stole a kiss and she stole my heart in front of her house on the same street. But on that Saturday in May, we agreed before God and our families and assembled congregation to begin the journey of bearing witness to each other's lives. It has been a joyful journey.

Sometimes, however, the journey has brought hardship, pain, tears and grief. It is for better or worse and we promised. But really Christian marriage is much a much deeper testimony that just two people looking into the deepest recesses of their soul. It is also a testimony, lived out before God for others to bear witness also. It is Christ and the church, His beloved Bride, and their unending bond.

Tonight I want to stand before you, my beloved church family, and you my children and family, and you who knew Pam well and bear witness to the faithfulness of God to us as a couple, even when the fire was hot and seemed only to get hotter.

Pam was, as the Bible describes, a godly, submissive wife. She was not a pushover or doormat. If you have worked in a surgical suite with her, you pretty much knew who ran the room...no matter what the doctor thought. She was strong willed and determined... a trait that didn't leave her even toward the end of her life.

And she willingly submitted to me even when God called me to ministry and then, three months later, to sell everything we owned and move into the hills of Appalachia where I would attend college for the next two years. She submitted to me again when I uprooted her and moved her further still to Louisville Ky where I would spend the next decade in seminary and where we would become parents. And her submission would be deeper still when we uprooted our family at God's beckoning to serve a church that was exactly 760 miles from her parent's driveway...in Jacksonville Florida. It is not that she didn't have opinions about those decisions and ultimately they were made with her input and approval...but she submitted what she wanted first in trust that I was hearing from and following God's leadership. And she knew that I loved her.

Pam beautified Christ in the way she lived her life personally, spiritually, and in relationships. The fragrance of Christ followed her around like the Estée Lauder "Beautiful" cologne she loved to wear.

But the hardest submission of our lives together took place in April as the diagnosis of a glioblastoma rocked our world. Through all of this...all of this...the light of Jesus shone through her even as her fragile "jar of clay" was crushed by the cancer. Yet in all of this she *trusted in the faithfulness of her "good, good Father" and through the pain, the despair, and indignity of it all she never took her eyes off of Him. She submitted to His will, even though submission meant drinking the bitter cup of suffering and the dying of her flesh and even though we and many others worldwide were praying as did Jesus, "Father let this cup pass from us."*

I want to say again, I am bearing witness to her faithfulness as she endured to the end a battle I could not imagine and she did so filled with faith. Even when we realized toward the last few weeks that the cancer had returned and her physical limitations were worse even than before, she trusted...she submitted as did the holy women of old...even if it meant that God would not deliver her in the way we had hoped and prayed. We have repeated numerous times that, through all of us, we have never...NEVER...felt closer to God.

For me, I have received the greatest privilege a Christian man can receive...to spend the last months of our journey together caring for my bride. "As Christ loved the church and gave Himself for her.." I received a rare gift...to show my wife with words and without how much I loved her. To serve her as a Christian husband is to serve. To wash her feet literally and figuratively... every day. To care for her with everything I had. I am grateful beyond words for a church body that allowed me that high and holy privilege.

She asked me once, "Tim, do you miss being at church on Sunday and preaching?" And I will tell you how I answered her. "Every moment of every day we are preaching the greatest sermon I have ever had the privilege to preach. And every moment, as we endure in this, we are being made more like Jesus for others to see.

Hours before Pam breathed her last, she awoke enough to speak. She would sometimes, as those suffering from this condition do, talk with people who weren't there. She would look right past us and see another world...an invisible one. She had spoken very little we could understand in the preceding days, and did not recognize us. On this day she opened her eyes, and she said "I see my Daddy...Uncle Franklin..." And then she began singing, "It is well...it is well...it is well with my soul....". And almost immediately, she said "Fix my hair." I believe in that moment Jesus was present in the room.

She never opened her eyes again. She never spoke another word...but earlier she said, "We have a good, good Father. Be sure Christ is glorified in my funeral. Make sure people know how to come to Him."

I stand today as a witness to a life well lived...a servant of Jesus who finished well...a wife who's value to me is " worth than precious jewels....more precious than rubies." In this season, I have never loved her more.

I also want to fulfill her request that you be given an opportunity to open your heart to the Father Who brought us together and Who carried us through this storm. He is a good, good Father Who loved us, Who took mercy and pity on us in our lostness and sin, and Who sent His only begotten Son as a substitute for the punishment we deserved. ` *Jesus said "I am the Way, the Truth, and the Life...and no man comes to the Father but by Me."*

The singing and tears continued for several moments again, since we agreed the way we would most honor her was through the music that meant so much to her. Each song spoke volumes to those who knew her well, and expressed her faith through the years and through this trial.

Glen Owens did, as expected, an amazing job proclaiming Christ and speaking about Pam for me. He and his wife Susan had walked with us for the past several years through my service to Florida Baptists on the State Board of Missions and more recently as president. He had mentored me for several years as an "executive coach." I had told him earlier, "Glen, Pam and I need a pastor. Now. You have to do it." He graciously agreed.

From his remarks, I will never forget his saying this one thing. He said, "Pam's faithfulness in this trial, even unto death, completes every sermon her husband has preached for the past thirty-five years of their ministry. Watching them in this time, you know that every word he spoke was truth. God is real. He is with us."

And then, just like that, the service had ended. I didn't want it to be over. But two hours had passed, an unheard of length of time for a funeral. And the spirit in the auditorium, even through the tears, was a spirit of revival! It was surprisingly not draining....but energizing.

I'm not sure what frame of mind I expected to be in when

the last song began. Broken? Weeping? Unable to stand? I had struggled thinking about this moment. Sitting just a few feet away from the casket bearing Pam's body, though I knew she was truly not there, still kept me close to her.

As we had said early in our courtship, we didn't want to ever be apart. As my children and their spouses and I walked out, we followed the bier carrying her body to the hearse that would bear her earthly tent away. I then asked the director for the privilege of doing one more thing ... I opened, and closed the door for my sweetheart one last time.

> *I know You're able, and I know You can*
> *Save through the fire with Your mighty hand;*
> *But even if You don't*
> *My hope is in You alone.*
> *I know the sorrow and I know the hurt,*
> *Would all go away if You'd just say the word*
> *But even if You don't,*
> *My hope is in You alone.*
> *It is well, it is well*
> *It is well with my soul. — (MercyMe, "Even If")*

Guest Blog: David Tarkington, First Baptist Church, Orange Park Fl.

As a pastor, I have the great privilege of bringing words of comfort and as a church family (First Baptist Church of Orange Park) we have been praying for our sister church across the St. Johns River here in Jacksonville at Fruit Cove Baptist Church. Earlier this year, Pam Maynard, wife of Pastor Dr. Tim Maynard, was diagnosed with cancer. On Saturday morning, August 5, I received a text message from Dr. Rick Wheeler, our Lead Missional Strategist for the Jacksonville Baptist Association, that Pam had died.

Pam's funeral service was scheduled for yesterday, Tuesday, August 8 at 7pm at Fruit Cove. My wife, Tracy, and I attended. The sanctuary of the church was packed with standing room only. Hundreds of friends, family members, church members, and representatives from sister churches, the Florida Baptist Convention, Mayo Hospital, and numerous other places were there.

The service was streamed on the church's website as many from Pam's home state of Kentucky as well as other places around the world tuned in to be a part of the service.

As I said earlier, I have been to many funeral services. I have preached at most of them. On this occasion, I was there because of my friend and fellow pastor and his family and church as they honored the life of this dear woman and saint.

Numerous men spoke from the pulpit this evening. The surgeon Pam served under and with while working as an orthopedic surgery nurse at Mayo spoke. Dr. Neal Cordle, Executive Pastor at FCBC, Dr. Glen Owens, formerly of the Florida Baptist Convention and now an active member at FCBC, Pastor Patrick Martin, son-in-law of Tim and Pam, and Dr. Maynard himself.

When Tim spoke, he did so as a husband of 40

years to Pam. At first declaring that he may not have the strength to finish his portion of speaking, it was soon clear that God enabled Tim to proclaim clearly and strongly of his love for Pam and of God's strength and power. The message was more than just heart-felt, it was anointed. Tim may never fully realize this side of heaven the impact that short, fifteen-minutes of speaking has had upon those in attendance and watching via livestream. It was stated last night and I agree - Tim and Pam's journey these past few months culminating with this pointed celebration of life and God's goodness was the very best sermon he ever has had the privilege of preaching. To God be the glory.

A worship service took place on a rainy Tuesday night in St Johns County this week. A packed building with hundreds in attendance including perhaps fifty pastors erupted in an honorable, blessed, focused service of worship to the one and only God.

Brian Woofter and the FCBC Celebration Choir and Orchestra led us to the throne of God in singing and worship. The organ remained unplayed as Pam had served in that role for years. Flowers sitting upon the instrument reminded everyone of this act of service (just one of many) that Pam offered her Lord and church. Jason Lovins, a gifted singer and virtually adopted son (Pam called herself Jason's "Florida mom") spoke briefly and sang praises to the God of hope and healing.

Two hours after the welcome, the service ended and Pam's casket was wheeled out of the building. Two hours in a service on a rainy Tuesday...and it could've continued even longer.

A Most Excellent Funeral

A most excellent funeral for a most excellent wife (Proverbs 31).

God was glorified. He alone was worshipped this evening.

Pam was honored.

Tim and family were and are being comforted by the only One who can truly do so.

There were tears shed.

There were poignant moments.

There was laughter.

The Gospel was shared clearly.

Life was celebrated.

Yesterday was remembered and tomorrow declared, as Pam's body may no longer live, but she does because of Christ.

We were all reminded that it is good to go to funerals every now and then (Ecclesiastes 7:2).

I worshipped with my brothers and sisters. It was sweet. It was bittersweet, to be honest. Yet, it was right.

Our Father smiled.

And that was a most glorifying funeral.

REFLECTIONS ON
A LIFE WELL LIVED

I have thought much about the previous section. My first inclination was not to be totally, brutally honest. I will still leave some of that honesty and transparency for another time. My decision was to follow the tracks of the Gospel writers who, inspired by the Holy Spirit, elected to describe the crucifixion with an economy of words and to leave much of the graphic details to other sources. There are good reasons to do that, and so I have chosen an economy of words for my sharing of our testimony.

For now, I simply want it recorded and remembered that I am fulfilling a promise I made to Pam. A promise to tell our love story, for the few or the many who would care to read it...but mostly for our sweet McCail...and to bear witness to the reality that, truly, though our bodies fail and death does separate us for a time, "love never fails."

I must also take this moment to bear witness to the genuineness of a community of Jesus-loving church folks who I am privileged to pastor, who extended their love, care, food, prayers, and lent me their hope in our time of deepest heartbreak. If anyone ever doubted the reality of the living Christ, immersing them in Christian community will empty their minds of any such doubt. This is a love that goes beyond the pale...true "agape"... beyond normal. It is a transcending, eternal love motivated by more than just sympathy or pity. It is a love motivated by, saturated in, fragranced by the presence of the Living Christ Himself. It was and is God loving me tangibly and fully through their arms, their eyes, their generosity, service and their caring. It took the form of more cards and letters and emails and text messages than could be counted; and of a church family that provided more than one hundred and ten days of meals in a row. It could be explained in no other way than to say...God did it. God is real and He did this. And He alone should receive the glory!

Final Update – August 14

One thing that continues to resonate within me is an overwhelming gratitude for all that God has done through so many during this difficult season culminating in Pam's Homegoing. It is beyond "being thankful." It is actually a gratitude beyond words.

My daughter is laboring in the room next to me, writing thank-you notes to so many who sent gifts and flowers and memorials for Pam. Our family long ago banned me from writing due to my terrible penmanship, which would probably not let me pass elementary school. (Sorry Mrs. Ross at Charles Russell Elementary).

So I will attempt to speak a gratitude that defies

the barriers of language on behalf of my family. Many, many people ought to be personally thanked for the faithfulness and generosity shown us through this most difficult of times. She would insist that I try.

We have been blessed by flowers, gifts and food (skillfully and lovingly coordinated by Shelly Rabon and the Meal Train ministry) providing us with meals worthy of the greatest episodes of the Food Channel.

Our stomachs have been filled even though our hearts have been breaking through the days since Pam's April 17 surgery. And please know that, in our neighborhood filled with many who are unchurched, the unwavering care and devotion you showed day by day did not go unnoticed. They have seen through your love what the body of Christ really looks like. You showed up... some to simply sit and pray... and it mattered.

Your prayers for us and for Pam's healing have bombarded the gates of Heaven and been laid as a pleasing incense before the Father's throne of grace. We have seen this daily through the Prayers for Pam website. In His Sovereignty and in fatherly wisdom He chose to bring her home and answer our prayers for healing in His Presence. I longed for it to be otherwise... but submit to His grace and purpose for us in this.

As we have walked this journey, your church staff has stepped up in ways both seen and unseen to minister to us, and to you. We have been recipients of the care and blessings and talents they have shared, as you have, through these difficult days.

We are grateful beyond words for the sacrificial gifts and kindness of so many. But I would like again to mention the selfless sacrifice of time, attention and care offered by Tanya and Tim Klein. Tanya's relationship with and care and love for Pam was remarkable and refreshing. She was, I believe, sent by God for such a time as this. Our family's gratitude and love for their selfless gift to us is beyond measure and could never be repaid.

I shared in another post that Psalm 40:1-3 was our "guide" and spiritually "framed" this experience for us. As we cried out to the Lord expectantly and patiently, He heard our cry and answered. Pam's feet, once buried in the muddy "pit" of cancer, are now firmly standing on the solid rock. He sustained and carried us, as we prayed and as we waited, in the struggle of our pain and circumstance.

That leads me to my final note of gratitude... our family's thankfulness for the service of celebration last Tuesday night. I have never been anywhere in my lifetime where the presence of the Lord was so real... where the sweetness of Heaven was so evident... and the "temporary troubles" of this present day faded into such glory. But I should not be surprised; because Psalm 40:3 assured us it would happen. "And many will see and fear and put their trust in the Lord." Praise God, that night they did.

And for that, we will be forever grateful beyond words.

So much of the grace I received in this valley came through the constant love, and care, and presence of our children. Allison and Patrick, Dave and Logan and, of course, little McCail poured so much oil into our wounds by their presence and love. It's wonderful to have children in your home, but when they become adults that you love and respect and lean on and who, as I mentioned earlier, sometimes even need to "parent" you, it is even more wonderful. They never let us down, even for a moment, during this trial. It's easy to lose your way in the darkness of this kind of experience. Our children brought light to our path.

Pam's sisters, Debbie Vicini and Tracey Harr, came for a refreshing visit before Pam's condition worsened to the point of her inability to receive them. They found the visit a time of joyful, tearful celebration...and closure. I will never forget the difficulty of their leaving each other that weekend.

My brother Mark and sister-in-law Beth visited with us for a few days; a time which became something of a revival and prayer meeting for us all. During their stay we managed for the first time to get Pam successfully into the pool laying on a raft. We all rejoiced with tears seeing her floating in the water, hoping it would be the first of many times. It was the first of only two. But the moment provided at least at the time, a much-needed victory. Both Mark and Beth spoke words of faith and healing into our lives. I will never outlive my gratitude for them.

And in the midst of this season, a lady named Tanya Klein walked into Pam's room at Brooks Rehabilitation, simply stating "I'm here...and I'm all in." Tanya had done this once before, when Pam broke a knee in a biking accident a few years before. She worked with us during that time virtually every day for five months. She brought with her an experience in rehabilitation, an amazing resilience, and an unshakeable positive attitude that kept me and Pam moving forward.

Although her journey with us this time was just over three months in total, I'm sure at times it seemed much longer to her. Every day she showed up and wouldn't let us quit. She had to get in my and Pam's face at times, and did it with firmness but also with grace. She managed the incredible supply of food that came to our house from the church family. I will never be able to thank her and her husband Tim adequately for the sacrifices they made for us in this ordeal. She literally was a daily reminder of the unfailing presence of God and the love of the body of Christ through this trial. I will forever have "a new sister" in Tanya.

God never let us go. He did not fail. I bear witness to that. He did exceedingly more than we could have asked or imagined, a promise we claimed throughout. And He kept His promises. All of them. He never let us walk through the fire alone, and that was what He promised. I have every confidence that every tear shed, every anxious thought, every pain of disease or loss was felt and will be remembered by our good, good Father. Every tear is kept and counted by Him. None were wasted.

In that truth I rest my hope.

PART 7

MOVING BEYOND

Tim and Pam had a life of love for God, family and each other that was an example to anyone watching.

Tim and family together on first Christmas without Pam.

KEEP WALKIN'

**The Way is Narrow and the Path is Steep —
August 25, 2017**

*"The way is narrow and the path is steep
Lord keep me walkin, walkin, "*

-David Crowder, "Keep Me"

Spiritual pilgrimages are nothing new. The imagery of the Christian walk as a pilgrimage of sorts is sprinkled throughout the New Testament. We "walk" by faith, not by sight. We "walk" with Jesus. We "walk" in the spirit. I am trying to "walk" on this journey in obedience to God... looking for clarity in the fogginess of grief.

I am on a quest. My quest is an answer to the question, "what's next?" I can't "return to normal." I have been changed in fundamental ways by Pam's death and the months preceding it.

I have told people dozens of times through the years, as a pastor, that when a trauma such as divorce, or death or job loss or radical health change comes we go on a quest for a "new normal" because, like it or not, "old normal" cannot be regained.

So like millions have done through the years, I am returning to sites holy to me. This must begin in my hometown. Though I am here in Ashland, Ky on one level to attempt to serve my mother and Pam's family in the chaos following her father's death, I am also attempting to make sense of the chaos that at times envelopes my spirit and emotions.

The bearings of my life that helped me stay focused are sometimes hard to spot in the turbulence of change that comes in the wake of loss. I realize both the peril and potential that are inherent in such a time as this. Sometimes I feel my feet are planted firmly on solid rock. Other times I feel like I'm in freefall. I am assured both are normal.

I have decided, guided I believe by the Holy Spirit, to return to the places in history and our life together, and give thanks for them: Our first home site (the trailer is long gone but not the barn full of chickens). A visit to the park where we would sometimes sit and talk into the "wee" hours and dream of our life together. After we married, we would go there and grab a quick supper on her evening shift break from the hospital and the end of my day at the phone company. The park where our children played, pushed on swings by their grandparents and munching snowcones from the concession stand.

I returned to the side "yard" (now parking lot) at the church where we were married in an outdoor garden ceremony, characterized by simplicity and beauty and the awareness of a new beginning. Little has changed physically in our hometown. Much hasn't changed at all! Memories flood back easily with these physical reminders and landmarks.

And along the way, I am meeting with spiritual mentors who initially shaped my understanding of God's call in my life to the pastorate. Though some have passed on to our truest Home, others remain. These are people I will seek out, since their initial counsel was valuable and true.

Next Sunday, I have agreed to visit my first pastorate in Shepherdsville, Ky for their 100th Homecoming. This is the place where my children met the Lord and were baptized, raised and found their initial spiritual experiences. The church was the tool God used to shape me and teach me how to pray and prepare three sermons a week. They suffered much under my early sermons. But they loved me anyway and I haven't seen them in 25 years.

Along the way, I have many who have reached out to me inviting me to connect with them as I "travel" through on this journey. I will try to connect with them.

As I go along, I have learned a hard lesson. You can't go home again. You change. Home changes. People change. Physical locations, if they still exist, decay and sometimes fall or are torn away. Change is only hard when you convince yourself you can somehow get along without it happening. But the only unchangeable in life is Jesus Christ, who is "the same yesterday, today, and forever."

Change comes because our Father doesn't want us ultimately hanging on to anything, anyplace or anyONE except Him in this earthly journey we are all on. While glimpses of heaven do come to us in the creation around us, it ultimately is fallen and we await "a new heaven and a new earth." Something better is on the way.

These days, that promise means more to me than it ever has.

When two become one, as Pam and I truly did over a marriage that lasted 14,682 days of life together, it becomes extremely difficult to extract one soul from the other. Pam and I knew each other so very well. We lived in each other's rhythms, we read each other's thoughts. Often, I would be silently thinking about a song, and she could come in singing aloud exactly where I was as it played inside my head. She knew when I was "off," when I was worried or down or distracted. She knew when I needed to retreat and be alone. She would gently prod and challenge me to take days off which now, much to my regret, I wish I had done more. We partnered together fully in the ministry God had entrusted to us and were blessed beyond measure by God in it.

When two become one, a mystery happens that only God

understands. It is a mystery like the relationship between Christ and His bride, the church. In her, I had found "the one whom my soul loved." We became soulmates in every sense this word could be humanly defined. The mystery was a reality to us.

During our months in the hospital and while convalescing at home, I felt my personal prayer life suffered. My habits were clearly thrown up in the air, and I found it difficult to find time to clear my thoughts enough to pray well, though I am confident that "the Spirit makes intercession for us," even when our words are just groans.

However, ironically, during this same period our time of spiritual growth together soared. We were never more "in sync" spiritually than in those weeks and months...indeed, incomparably precious times of communion with God and each other. It was an incredible gift that God gave us as we read the Bible, sought the Lord for others as well as ourselves, and truly worshiped on the deepest level. It was as though God was sealing us spiritually even as we were beginning to be torn apart physically and emotionally by her illness. Over and over, God fulfilled a promise to Pam.

Before her surgery, she had begun to read Priscilla Schirer's book entitled "God is Able." She finished the night before surgery. The theme of her book is that God is more than enough for whatever we are going through. When she finished reading, she felt impressed to lay claim to Ephesians 3:20-21, "Now to Him who is able to do exceeding abundantly and above all that we could ask or think according to the power that works within us, to Him be glory in the church by Christ Jesus to all generations, forever and ever, Amen." I agreed with her that these would be our anchor verses for the coming days, and they became our promise.

From Heaven's View – July 26

Perspective changes everything. A few years ago, my son and I had the opportunity to go on patrol with the Jacksonville Sheriff's Office helicopter unit. We flew over the city at night... and from the air it was breathtaking. Much different than the perspective of the city I have looking out my car window stuck in construction or rush hour traffic. Same city... different view.

Perspective changes everything. In 2008, a friend of mine gave me a book and said, "You need to read this. It really helped me through a tough time." Now this happens to me often. I just received a 608 page book from the author who wanted me to read and review it for him "in my spare time" (!)

The title my friend handed me in 2008, was written by T.W. Hunt and titled, From Heaven's View. It was a deep book and, at the time, one I felt unnecessary. But perspective changes everything.

And I have found myself these days very much in need of the insights in that volume. How do we manage and even find joy in times of sorrow, suffering and grief? By having the right perspective... for the Christian it is having a heavenly one.

From heaven's view, our trials can turn to gold. Our sufferings become the "filling up of the sufferings of

Christ." Our pain and hardship become "not worthy to be compared to the glory to be revealed." Our tears are kept in a bottle by God... not one is lost or wasted. Our time here... though moments may drag slowly by... is nothing to be compared to eternity awaiting us.

From heaven's view, our sorrows and struggles are used to "conform us to the image of Christ." Our suffering is not meant to crush us, but to create in us "endurance, and... endurance, hope."

From heaven's view, hope becomes not, "I hope so" but "I know so." Hope is not rooted in a desired change of circumstance, but in the unchanging character of our God who is the same "yesterday, today, and forever."

With heaven's view, we can press on and not lose heart. Every hurt, every disappointment, every sleepless night of pain and even persecution comes not to harm us but for our good and God's glory. (Romans 8:28). From heaven's view, even the cross does not end in defeat... but resurrection.

From heaven's view, all things work together... nothing is random, wasted, aimless, or amiss. From heaven's view, though weeping comes for a night, joy comes in the morning. From heaven's view, a perspective through our Father's eyes and God's sovereign throne....

...it can be well with our soul.

What is not yet clear to me is what happens when one of those inseparable people we call "soulmates" goes away...when the one who your soul loves is only with you in memories and pictures and empty echoes of a hollow house.

In the years I have officiated weddings and, in my own, I spoke the words "til death do you part." And yet, it is something you never really think about having to face...not in reality. That a day comes when the conversation of the past years is now silenced, and the one to whom your soul has been knit together is no longer with you.

Some have described grief as losing part of your own heart...your own soul. Indeed I feel very much like this has happened. It is like having to learn to eat, walk, think, even to breathe properly again.

After Pam's funeral, I felt the need to go on a "pilgrimage" of sorts. It took me back to places sacred to us...hallowed in my memories. These were places we had certainly seen and visited since our early days of dating and marriage, but this time they were filled with something far different. Not nostalgia...but a sweetness mixed with pain. Joyful tears and memories that were both cherished and hard to revisit. I traveled some roads seldom seen by us these past forty years, and along the way I sat with friends dear to both of us whom I sought out as I journeyed.

Three weeks were spent on the road, and a couple of thousand miles turned over on my odometer. I suppose there was a part of me that just wanted to spend the rest of my life driving and staring through my windshield. It was the only place my life made sense. But the day came that I had to face what I most dreaded...walking into our house for the first time alone.

This journey—only a few steps from my car and garage— was far longer than the thousands of miles I had just logged. A loneliness met me that I had never felt with such force. It was as though a tangible presence met me and as I entered the house. I heard the words "keep walkin'" in my head.

I walked from room to room, smelling familiar scents and viewing a house that was my home...but not. Many prayed for me in that moment of transition, and the presence of the Lord was sweet and real. But in that first few steps, I became aware that my journey was not ended...it had in reality just started.

The tears flowed freely, and I was torn with the thought of simultaneously trying to make things look different and, at the same time, not wanting to move or touch anything. I knew that, once I did, the importance of those things would never again be seen or experienced by me. Pam had lovingly selected, shopped, placed and decorated with these items of furniture and other items. I sometimes wondered if her fingerprints were still on them.

Grief takes more than a person from you. It takes much more. It takes the familiar, the normal, the comfortable routine, the moments that bring comfort and leaves in its place an aching void. A confusion. A lack of place. And lingering still is a nagging question: "What next?"

I looked at plants that I knew were not going to survive long under my care. I wondered when I needed to go the store, and how to do that without my list, even though I always returned home leaving something off of it. A thousand questions confronted me in those first minutes and hours back home.

After several moments, I called her mom and mine to tell them I was home safely. Both of our mothers are on this journey as well...my mom has been for fifteen years. Pam's mom began the previous year with the death of the last of her siblings, her husband months before and now, her middle daughter. They both are walking with me in this pain, and I know reliving their own grief as they do.

I find myself often thinking, "what would Pam want me to do right now?" And I try to act accordingly. I am left, as I have counseled so many in the past, with living one day...one minute... at a time. And I have found that grief leaves a gash...a huge, aching scar that divides your life "before the death" and "after the death." Hard and precious memories exist on one side of the scar...and questions and loneliness exist on the other.

I participate fully in life, I think. I have gone back to preaching and serving our wonderful church family, Fruit Cove Baptist. And though much of life for me and my children and family goes on like it did before all of this happened, everything seems odd to me. Like moving into a house where you don't know where to turn on the lights or where to find the things you need to function, I am having to think deeply about each step and each decision.

People have asked me directly, have asked my staff at work, have asked those who are closest to me, "what does pastor like to eat? To do?" And I have no answer. Those were questions I let Pam answer. We did what she wanted, what she liked because that was usually what I wanted too. Now she is not here to ask. These are things many people go through in grief. I am sure I am far from alone on this journey. It has many travelers on the path to resolution.

But while I sincerely wish to always honor our marriage, honor our relationship, and honor the life we made together, I don't wish to live trapped in a past I cannot return to or live in any longer.

(This blog post was written three months after Pam's death)

I'm on the road again this week, though this time not alone. I am traveling into some really cold weather with our happy group of about 50 traveling senior adults. They'll be alright until the temperatures dive into the low 30's tonight! We are going north, back to Kentucky to visit the Creation Museum and the Ark Experience in Northern Kentucky near Cincinnati Ohio, where it's cold. Where it's snowing....in OCTOBER!

I am traveling as the official "chaperone" of group, and as the "camp pastor." So far they are easier to keep up with than the last youth trip I found myself on. But I travel with an empty seat beside me. I wish Pam were on this trip. I really do. She loved fall weather and fall foliage. I know today she sees much more beauty today than I do....far more than I could "think or imagine."

And yet, I miss her. Every day. Every night. The house is full of empty echoes. Places where she should be. I walk into rooms expecting her to be there. Sometimes, as I listen to music or have the TV blaring aimlessly in the background, I imagine I can hear her voice.

I have moments of clarity when I can fully embrace that she is gone and I am still here, and life goes on. I'm told it gets better. I'm sure it will, though there are days that I wonder. So much of my adult life has been lived and seen through her eyes as well as my own. I haven't figured out yet how to sit at the kitchen table *and eat a meal by myself. I guess I don't want to accept that this is "normal" now.*

Social events are becoming more complex. I am beginning to experience the "fifth wheel" occasions which many who are single or widowed talk about. And I'm still trying to find my "fit."

Even church is hard, though it's wonderful to walk for a few hours with the "family of God." I've learned in the past six or seven months the depth of what it means to have such a family to walk with through the fire and trials that come to us all. But church was something "we" did together...and every corner and every song holds a memory.

A death is not much different than an amputation. You try and use an arm or leg that has been lost or removed, even when it isn't there. Your whole life was oriented around having two hands, two feet, And now, there's only one. So everything feels different, disorienting. Like having to learn to walk and feed yourself all over again.

And though I usually can contain or compartmentalize them, memories come sometimes at a furious speed. Some are wonderful and I weep. Some are hard and I want to forget, but they all seem tied together, so I can't cauterize one without doing the same to the others.

As I suspected, memories are tied inextricably to tangible things. Last weekend, we had several pastors and their wives on campus from partner countries and cities where our church has gone on mission trips. Two of the wives (I judged) were approximately Pam's size and I also knew they would appreciate some of the clothing in Pam's wardrobe. So accompanied by a good friend, they came to my home (I wasn't there) and had "Christmas" as they went through clothing and shoes in Pam's closet. Pam had actually talked about sending some of her things as a donation to Haiti so this was even better as they came here to select what they wanted. They sent me pictures wearing some of their favorites from Pam's wardrobe! It was both joyous and hard.

I find myself sometimes crying at inconvenient times. On a bike ride. In the gym. I miss her, and sometimes that thought overwhelms me like an ocean swell. And then, mercifully, it subsides in the same way and just as unpredictably.

I miss her when I look into the face of my granddarlin'. McCail, as you know, was the apple of Pam's eye, and her greatest sorrow as she realized she was not going to recovery from the cancer was that her granddaughter wouldn't know her. I promised her that, every time McCail looked in a mirror, she would see her grandmother's eyes looking back! But it is also true that every time I see or spend time with my sweet grand baby, I see her Mamaw looking back at me.

They say you can't hug memories but I wish I could. Saturday I found myself back in St Augustine for the first time since her passing. We have so many great memories in the oldest city. Restaurants we enjoyed, places where we would go for an overnight getaway, stores she like to shop.

I went there to be part of a wedding for a young man I deeply love. The wedding was great, but it reminded me in very vivid ways that I am alone. My wedding ring reminds me of that constantly, even as it reminded me of my love and commitment when she was with me. But Pam is no longer by my side. My bride has gone to an eternal home where I know...I know....I will see her again. But until then, I'm alone.

And yet, I am not lonely. My children have been wonderful to keep me forward focused, making me plan for outings and events. They include me in their plans, and I am daily reminded how great it is to be a father and grandfather, and that life must go on. I have many in our church family who regularly touch base in person, or electronically, and friends around the globe who love and pray for me. I am lonely. But not alone.

The One Who promised, "I will never leave you nor forsake you" is faithful to His Word. He has never left me...and this I also know. He has never failed one moment to walk with me "in the valley of the shadow of death," and no matter how dark it has gotten He still comes to bring light...and life....and hope.

And so, in response to you and the many who ask, "How are you doing?" I continue to respond, "I am grieving nicely." But I miss her. I'm learning to "walk on one leg." I'm finding "new normal" a piece and a day at a time. Some days I fall, but I try to fall forward and not backward.

And with God's help and your prayers, I will...and my family will....keep walking.

With great love from your pastor and fellow struggler....

Tim, Pam, Dave, Logan and McCail, the star of the show.

THE FIRST CHRISTMAS

I began writing the blogs and journaling that frame this book a few months before Pam passed away. While the journey still continues for me and my family, this book will end just a few days after Christmas... five months to the day after her passing..my first Christmas and New Years without Pam by my side in over forty-one years.

It has been difficult to know how to "be" in this season of the year, particularly. Many are expecting to find me collapsing in a pool of tears and sorrow, but I remember how I felt on my dad's first "Christmas in Heaven." I could not weep for him, even though I still missed him. I knew that Christmas was his favorite holiday (well, really, all of them were) but he especially loved Christmas. He had memorized most of the parts...male and female...in Handel's oratorio "The Messiah." He sang in community presentations of the work, and loved it above all other music.

Likewise, I find myself oddly unable to weep for Pam on this Christmas. Perhaps I should...perhaps I am emotionally exhausted and just can't find tears to cry. Or maybe, just maybe... it's the same thing that happened with my father—how can I weep knowing what she is seeing and hearing right now? What must Christmas in Heaven be like? I miss her terribly, but for the first time in this journey, I cannot "wish her back" to a world that still groans and weeps because of the sin our Savior came to the earth to remedy.

So with the continuing prayers and encouragement of many, I walk on. I must press on as God gives me strength. I have placed a comma at the end of my life on earth with my soulmate, but not a period...and not a question mark. I live for a "not yet;" a coming reunion that is more certain than anything else I know. Resurrection always follows a crucifixion, Nik Ripken reminds me. And as I go on I will live in the light of that resurrection and make the necessary adjustments to find "new normal," and to realize as much of the joy and contentment without Pam that I enjoyed with her...until that day the "not yet" becomes "now"and we are forever together...and never have to part.

I know this is what she would want me to do..."right to the end."

GRIEVING NICELY

(Written January 30, 2018)

A friend who is an author gently counseled me going into the writing of this book that I may be attempting it a little too soon. On some days, I believe he was right. The memories that I have tried to put on paper have torn holes in my soul again and again as I relived each of them. But then, when will be the time that grief does not have the power to do that to us?

Somehow thinking through it again and putting it in writing has helped me process some of the pain.

I have known academically and now, by daily experience, that grief is a mysterious and often unpredictable experience. It is not "linear," meaning it is not a clean, step-by-step predictable process. And just about the time you think you have passed into an easier season, something happens to pull you back.

It is an experience to endure...to walk through patiently day-by-day. You learn early on that there is no point in asking "how long" it will last. It will last until the final day that Jesus calls you home. The degree to which it lasts, however, does vary.

There are things that I have changed in our home....items I have given to family or friends or donated. But there are areas of the house that seem, for lack of a better word, "sacred." I can't touch those yet...can't even think about it. I'm sure in time I will be able to...but not yet.

I have gone back to work full time, and the church was gracious to give me some months away on sabbatical to heal and to write. Since coming back in early November, I have performed eight funerals...some for people I knew and some I did not. Oddly, I can get through those OK. But weddings...weddings I have not attempted yet.

My memory is crystal clear when thinking about our journey since April, and about mine and Pam's life together. But in spite of an iPhone, iPad and Libby Gillean, my very capable and wonderful ministry assistant, I am still forgetful. My counselor tells me that is to be expected.

The grief still "ambushes" me; a song in a store...a fragrance...a moment when someone in public looks like Pam at a glance...a picture that always hangs in the house but for some reason on some days reduces me to tears. That is the journey. I am told and believe it gets better.

In the meantime, I am "grieving nicely." My sister-in-law Beth who, along with my brother Mark, have given me refuge time after time through this experience, acquainted me with this phrase. It seems to capture how I truly feel when someone asks me how I'm doing and the day may have been hard. "Grieving nicely" is where I seem to be.

I am grateful not to be alone on the journey. My children

and their spouses, my granddaughter, my loving family and wonderful church make the days not only bearable....but joyful.

I have a promise that I claim and cling to often. Jesus said, "I will never leave you nor forsake you." (Hebrews 13:5)

And for me, that promise will always be enough.

Tim and McCail, the sunshine in his life.

ABOUT THE AUTHOR

D r. Tim Maynard has served as Senior Pastor of the Fruit Cove Baptist Church in St. Johns, Florida for the past twenty-five years. A native of Ashland, Kentucky, Tim loves biking, playing drums, and spending time with his granddarlin,' McCail. His daughter Allison lives in Russellville, Alabama, with her husband Patrick, also a pastor. His son Dave resides in St. Johns County where he teaches and chairs the Arts Department of Nease High School. Dave's wife, Logan, is in management with the Bank of America.

Treasure in Jars of Clay

7 But we have this treasure in jars of clay, to show that the surpassing power belongs to God and not to us. **8** We are afflicted in every way, but not crushed; perplexed, but not driven to despair; **9** persecuted, but not forsaken; struck down, but not destroyed; **10** always carrying in the body the death of Jesus, so that the life of Jesus may also be manifested in our bodies. **11** For we who live are always being given over to death for Jesus' sake, so that the life of Jesus also may be manifested in our mortal flesh. **12** So death is at work in us, but life in you. **13** Since we have the same spirit of faith according to what has been written, "I believed, and so I spoke," we also believe, and so we also speak, **14** knowing that he who raised the Lord Jesus will raise us also with Jesus and bring us with you into his presence. **15** For it is all for your sake, so that as grace extends to more and more people it may increase thanksgiving, to the glory of God. **16** So we do not lose heart. Though our outer self is wasting away, our inner self is being renewed day by day. **17** For this light momentary affliction is preparing for us an eternal weight of glory beyond all comparison, **18** as we look not to the things that are seen but to the things that are unseen. For the things that are seen are transient, but the things that are unseen are eternal.

2 Corinthians 4:7-18

The Love of God

35 Who shall separate us from the love of Christ? Shall tribulation, or distress, or persecution, or famine, or nakedness, or danger, or sword? **36** As it is written, "For your sake we are being killed all the day long; we are regarded as sheep to be slaughtered." **37** No, in all these things we are more than conquerors through him who loved us. **38** For I am sure that neither death nor life, nor angels nor rulers, nor things present nor things to come, nor powers, **39** nor height nor depth, nor anything else in all creation, will be able to separate us from the love of God in Christ Jesus our Lord.

Romans 8:35-39

—————— POSTSCRIPT ——————

BY MARK MAYNARD
THEY WILL ALWAYS BE MY HEROES OF THE FAITH

My brother and I were darn crafty in our dating days. While neither of us were Casanovas, we were able to do the improbable:

We married up. Yes, you might say we outkicked the coverage — by a mile — and got way better than we deserved.

God smiled on both of us, Tim with his darling wife Pam and me with my sweetheart Beth. Neither of us make it this far without them. That's a pure fact.

Tim and I never had much in common. He was into the heavy-metal music scene and I was into sports. I hung out with friends his age probably more than he did. He played the tuba in band; I listened to "Band on the Run." He played drums with Coco the Clown. I played baseball with the neighborhood gang.

Our wives, while different in many ways, had a lot of similarities — striking similarities. You can't make this stuff up.

Both Pam and Beth are middle sisters with an older sister and a much younger one (12 years in both cases.) Their fathers were both Hall of Fame-type workers for Ashland Oil, carrying the kind of respect you'd hope to someday earn in whatever job you work.

Their mothers were (and still are for that matter) homemakers who could do anything and Beth's mother did some teaching (all three of her girls are teachers as well, to the surprise of no one). And when it comes to cooking, Alva Boggs and Shirley Sloas cooked it up better than anybody. I mean, seriously, just look at me. Tim and I stand as (full-bellied) testaments to that fact since we have eaten their cooking and the cooking of their daughters (who cook just like them) for years.

Pam and Beth grew up in homes that put God ahead of all else. They learned by watching their godly parents and their lives were guided by those principles. They had perfect role models.

Tim and I grew up in the same kind of home, and in the same church where the Sloas family attended in Catlettsburg.

Dad's 'girls'

My father loved Pam so much he was determined that one of his boys would make her his bride. Tim took him up on it. But here's another similarity: When Dad met Beth, he fell in love with her, too. She was so much more than a daughter-in-law to him. During his last year of life, she faithfully paid visits and took short walks with dad during the summer. He looked forward to that time as much as he did the sun coming up. They grew eternally close.

Here's something else Pam and Beth have in common: Compassion for others and sweet, sweet spirits. They would make others comfortable before themselves, a product of being the daughters of Leonard Sloas and Fred Boggs.

I can remember visiting Tim and Pam in Cumberland on the drive home from Florida in 1980 after I'd proposed to Beth. They were so excited when I told them the news. Pam was like the big sister I never had. She treated me like the little brother she never had.

Once I married Beth, I gained two more of the most wonderful "sisters" anyone could ask. But Pam was first, since Tim was married before me.

Fight night?

The love that Tim and Pam had for each other was obvious from the start.

Tim likes to tell the story of how late one Saturday night her old boyfriend was waiting out in front of our house after Tim and Pam had been on a date. Tim was faced with the reality that a fight might be about to happen and, let's just say, Tim was more lover than fighter (remember, he was a drummer). But when my friends and I came rolling up about 10 strong, Tim was never so glad to see us (and he usually wasn't glad to see us).

"What's going on, Tim, everything OK?" I asked.

The ex-boyfriend backpedaled back to his car, saying, "Well, I'm not going to fight the whole gang!" My friends looked at each other and shrugged. Tim and Pam never heard from him again.

Brotherly love

Even though separated by hundreds of miles as Tim's ministry settled in Florida and my life settled here, we have grown even closer over the years, especially the last 10 or so. He is a confidante for me, my hero really, and so is Pam, who always knows the right thing to say. She was the epitome of a pastor's wife, oozing with sweetness and encouragement but not afraid to share her opinion. Sometimes you need that too. She was also a talented musician and surgical RN who has comforted thousands of patients.

We've laughed and we've cried together. They have shared our pain and our joy. The months of Pam's illness, we shared their ultimate pain and her eventual death that cut us to the quick. About six weeks before her death, we had a revival-like prayer service for them that was something else. It was a spiritual awakening in my soul that I'll never forget. My wife would say the same.

Meanwhile, we still pray, because that's what we were taught to do. We know who still sits on the throne. We pray and look toward God for help and understanding. Tim is healing and probably will for the rest of his life. But, through God's grace, he is indeed grieving nicely, to borrow a phrase from a friend of ours who lost her husband at a young age.

Pam will never be far from our hearts. Not now or ever. She made a permanent impression on anybody she met. And their love story, one that was centered around God and never wavered, even during the darkest of the days, will be one that is never-ending.

CPSIA information can be obtained
at www.ICGtesting.com
Printed in the USA
LVOW13*0950090318
569217LV00002B/2/P